Sticks and Stones
A Father's Journey Into Autism

Hank Smith

This Autistic Life
KELSEYVILLE, CALIFORNIA

This Autistic Life
4622 Lagoon Drive
Kelseyville, CA/95451
www.thisautisticlife.com

Book Layout ©2013 BookDesignTemplates.com

Sticks and Stones/ Hank Smith. -- 1st ed.
ISBN-13: 978-1511403580

Dedicated to...
My wife, Michelle, without her there'd be nothing.
My daughter, Kaylee, for her courage, patience, and acceptance.
And to Ian, who changed my life.

Thank you to...
Donna Hardy for planting the seed,
Marion Wentzien for watering it,
and to Kimberly Bowcutt for pruning the result.

Thanks also to…
Valerie Gardner and Nancy Brier for support and
encouragement,
Arden Hyatt and Charlene Norwood for Friday afternoons,
Jan Styles and Jen Conrad for initial editing,
and David Hyatt for a beautiful cover.

A Beginning

"Hank, I think my water just broke," Michelle said, her voice strangely calm.

It was an early morning in March. I was in the shower. I had a busy day ahead. My kindergarteners were singing a few songs for their parents that day, and my mind was miles away.

"Are you sure?"

"Well, it's not like I've done this before . . . would you come look?"

I turned off the water and climbed out of the shower. Michelle was standing there in the warm mist.

"They said in the childbirth class to smell it. If it doesn't have a smell, that means my water broke."

I felt very odd, kneeling there on the bathroom floor, sniffing at this small, mysterious puddle.

"I don't think it smells. You smell it."

Michelle awkwardly lowered herself to the floor, tucking her long brown hair behind her. "I don't smell anything."

Our Springer Spaniels decided to join in the act. Since the day we'd rescued them from the pound, I'd always called them our "baby warm-ups." What a wonderful picture—me, Michelle, and two excited dogs—down on the bathroom floor sniffing at the puddle, trying to decide whether our lives were about to change forever.

I called the doctor. "We think the water broke."

"What do we do now?" Michelle asked on the other phone.

"Well, Michelle, you're closer to the hospital at school than at home . . . the baby shouldn't come for hours yet. You should be fine at school if you want to go."

Michelle also teaches kindergarten, and it was typical of her to go ahead with her day. I wasn't so sure. We were heading out the door when I had a sudden thought.

"You're not teaching your clogging class this afternoon are you?"

Michelle also teaches clogging, a very vigorous dance similar to tap. I could just picture her pounding her way through the contractions on the dance floor.

"Of course not!" She paused, and then, "I'm kind of scared . . . excited, but scared."

"Me too."

I pulled her close, feeling the firm warmth of her swollen belly. "I love you."

"Love you too."

***

The call came in the middle of my kindergartners' performance. Michelle was on her way to the hospital. Greg, her school's principal, was driving her. I apologized to the parents, said goodbye to my kids, and ran from the room. They seemed almost as excited as I was.

I got stuck behind every slow driver in the world and discovered that no one pulls over when you honk and flash your headlights at them. I arrived at the hospital a few minutes behind the doctor. Michelle was already in the birthing room. Greg seemed vastly relieved to see me. Michelle was almost ready to start pushing, and I'm sure he was preparing himself to find out more than he ever really wanted to know about one of his best teachers.

The labor nurse was getting things ready. She turned to me and asked, "Do you have names picked out yet?"

"If it's a boy, Ian," I replied.

"I know this band where the singer's name is Ian, Ian Anderson," the nurse said.

"Yea, Jethro Tull. I just saw them down in San Francisco," I said. We were having a great discussion about Ian Anderson and his band Jethro Tull when I felt a hand squeezing my arm—hard.

"Talk about that later," Michelle said through gritted teeth. Ian was born around fifteen minutes later.

"Look at those fingers," I said to my exhausted wife. "He's starting guitar lessons before he learns to talk."

"I don't know," she laughed. "With those legs, he might be a dancer."

"Well, whatever he turns out to be, he was almost born without me," our doctor said. "You're quick!"

***

I sat there beside the bed in the silence of that evening. It was as though the entire hospital had stopped and, for this moment, held its collective breath. Michelle was asleep. In the soft glow of the bedside lamp she looked lovely—peaceful and infinitely content.

My new son lay sleeping in my arms . . . so helpless, so perfect, so beautiful.

I don't know if I'm responsible enough to have kids, I thought, as I pulled up to the hospital the next morning in a borrowed car.

We were bringing Ian home today, and the only working vehicle we owned was Michelle's two-seater sports car, it was not big enough for a family of three.

I had lived for years quite happily with a series of objects that I suppose, with a stretch of the imagination, one might call cars. If they started up when I asked them to and if the noises from the engine could still be drowned out by music, I was content. They all broke down with some regularity, and as a result, I'd seen many parts of California I would never have seen otherwise as I sat there alongside the road waiting for a ride, my car gently smoking in the background.

"We really need a good family car," Michelle often said during her "nesting period" while pregnant with Ian. "Especially since you don't have the slightest idea how to fix one."

The last thing I had any interest in buying was a new car. I managed to purchase new guitars and other musical equipment fairly frequently, but cars were a low priority. I regretted my selfish ways as I sheepishly pulled up to the hospital in my parents' van.

I had the radio on, a Bay Area news station that my father liked listening to. A reporter was going on about the housing prices in Silicon Valley, prices far beyond the reach of our two-teacher salary. We had bought our first house about a year ago, and I thought again how lucky we were to live where we did.

We live in Lake County, a few hours north of San Francisco. Tourism, pears, and wine are what bring most of the money to the county; thankfully, the winding mountain roads leading in keep us small and somewhat isolated from the city. I had moved here, kicking and screaming, from the Bay Area for my first teaching job. But now that I was starting a family, I knew I was in the right place.

I found a parking spot, and as I climbed out and closed the car door, I realized suddenly that I was scared again. A monumentally huge responsibility awaited me behind the clean, white walls of the hospital. Behind those walls, in a room made up to look like someone's bedroom—if you could forget the sharp odor of disinfectant and the cold metallic gleam of the machinery discreetly shoved to one corner—in that room my wife and son waited for me with life-changing patience.

It was a beautiful morning. It had rained before dawn, and the sky glowed a newly washed blue between the storm clouds. A flock of pelicans took off from the lake, snow white against the sky. I took a moment to stand there, gazing out at the lake. I breathed the cold, crisp, rain-scented air, pulling it deep into my lungs. And as I stood there, I felt my fears ease a little. I turned and headed into the hospital.

***

It was quiet as we pulled into our oak-shaded driveway: quiet until Cooter and Sebastian saw us. Banshee-like howls greeted me as I opened the car door. Our dogs always manage to make us feel like gods when we arrive home; they grovel and then prance about in turn, howling all the while as if we've been gone for years.

I opened the door to the backyard, and they came pouring into the house in a black and white wave, managing to make themselves look like a pack of ravening hounds instead of two medium-sized dogs. I sat down in my chair and let them have a look at Ian. They took a few sniffs, and after a couple of slobbery licks, they threw themselves to the floor at my feet and promptly went to sleep. Ian dozed off as well.

It was quiet again, but for the snoring of the dogs. Ian stirred in his sleep, his lips quivering as if he were nursing. Michelle dropped onto the couch with a sigh.

"Well, here we all are," she said.

I smiled as I sat there, my new son sleeping in my arms, my dogs snoring beside me, and Michelle; after the violent beauty of childbirth, there was Michelle—tired—but happy and healthy, beautiful and serene. Nothing was different, Michelle was still Michelle, and my dogs were still at my feet. We had simply added Ian to the equation, and he fit in perfectly.

Yes, here we all are, I thought. *We're home.*

{ 2 }

Preschool

I don't think we intentionally ignored the signs. Ian was our first child, and many of his idiosyncrasies were at first cute in an odd sort of way.

One of the first I remember was his fascination with the washing machine. Somehow he managed to figure out how to hold down the lid sensor button with his finger so he could have the lid up. When he'd hear the washer start, he'd come running with a footstool, clamber up and open the lid. He'd stand there for most of the cycle, his little diapered butt sticking out as he leaned over to watch the swirling maelstrom of color.

Another oddity was his obsession with vacuuming, now sadly in the past.

He used to love vacuuming and was actually quite good at it. For a blissful year or so, we had the cleanest floors around without having to lift a finger.

But time moved on, and the clouds began to gather on the horizon.

***

I could hear Michelle crying as she came into the house.

"Chelle? Chelle . . . come here. What's wrong, how did it go?"

She came in and sat on the edge of the bed, her beautiful doe-like eyes were soft with tears. I could hear Ian puttering off to his room.

"Are you okay? What happened?" I asked.

She brushed her long, golden-brown hair from her eyes. "They wouldn't take him."

"What? What do you mean 'they wouldn't take him'?"

"They said he didn't fit in. He couldn't sit to listen to a story . . . there was other stuff too, but basically they just don't think he can handle it."

"So you're saying he didn't make it into preschool? Everyone makes it into preschool!"

"Not Ian, I guess."

Things began to change that day as we sat there on our bed. I held Michelle close, kissed her tears, and tasted the salt; the first bitter drops of the rains to come.

{ 3 }

ABC's

When the ABC table arrived, my first reaction was, Oh God, where are we supposed to put it? But it was a Christmas gift from Grandma Doris, so there was no question about not keeping it. The table found a home in the corner of our kitchen and a place in Ian's heart. It was a small, square table with a multi-colored alphabet going around the outside edge. From the day I put it together, Ian was obsessed. He would come running into the kitchen in his onesie, sliding to a stop in front of the table, and point to a letter.

"Da?"

"That's 'E', Ian . . . the letter 'E'."

And off he'd go, back to his room muttering, "E, E."

Soon he'd be back again, "Da?"

"That one's called 'W'."

Often he would take my hand, guide me to the table, and point to the letters he knew; his dark eyes huge and solemn, voice somber. The alphabet was his church, and the table his bible.

He especially loved the letter "G." He'd run around the house yelling, "G", "G", but when he'd actually see one in print, it was cause for great celebration.

"G!" He'd scream. "Da . . . 'G'!" The rest of the day would be "G-Day," very festive if one has never experienced it.

Before we knew it, our two-year old son knew the names of all the letters of the alphabet. Michelle and I are both teachers, and we took a lot of ribbing from our friends who assumed we were pushing our son to be some academic prodigy.

But as I look back, I realize the table for what it was, yet another excuse. "He can't really talk yet, but he knows his ABC's."

We had become adept at finding anything that seemed 'normal' about our son, finding any excuse to put off the inevitable; anything to put off that bitter truth that some as yet unacknowledged part of us already knew.

He loved books too, just like other children. We kept his books in an old wooden crate. Michelle and I love to read, and we wanted to encourage that in Ian, so soon the crate was overflowing. Ian had seven or eight favorites which we read so often that I had many of them memorized. The images of those books come spilling back to me all these years later, *Baby's Boat*, *Grandfather Twilight*, *Owl Babies*— they are like old friends. My friend, Tom, painted a picture for Ian's room entitled "Choose Five Books." That was our bedtime mantra, "Choose five books, Ian."

***

Ian comes to me with his books. It is getting late, and I'm tired. I sit down in my old, worn chair, pull Ian onto my lap, and begin to read.

"Once upon a time, there were three baby owls, Sarah, Percy, and Bill."

Ian's blanket is wrapped in his fist, and he rubs it against his cheek as he sucks his thumb. His golden hair is soft, his body warm, and he smells of sleep. The day drifts away with the familiar words. The house is dark and silent, as we sit in the golden glow of the lamp.

Perhaps a storm blows outside, but we are safe here: safe and warm. The future, and what it may contain, is out there with the storm, held at bay by three baby owls.

{ 4 }

Within

It had been a long day. Michelle was already asleep. I'd sent her to bed as soon as we'd finished dinner. The baby was due in a few weeks, and she was exhausted. Ian, already in his pajamas, sat in front of the television. I felt vaguely guilty, letting my two-year-old zone out in front of that neon glow.

"Ian, it's time for bed. Let's turn the video off, and we'll go brush your teeth."

I was tired too, prepping for the school year was always draining. All I wanted was to get Ian into bed, read him a quick story, and to go join Michelle.

"Come on Ian, let's go." I turned off the television.

Ian picked up the remote and turned it back on.

"Ian, it's time for bed," I said reaching for the remote.

With a smirk, Ian put his hand behind his back. I took his arm and pulled the remote from his hand.

The rage was horrible. I watched as my beautiful son turned into a raging, spitting animal. Toys became weapons. Ian pounded them against my head and back as I forced him to the ground and held him there so he couldn't hurt himself. Ian's teeth sank into my arm, and my world became white heat, noise, and pain.

And then it was over. Ian returned, shaken and scared by what had happened. It was strangely quiet, but for our ragged breath and Ian's soft tears.

I found his blanket and doll, and Ian took them, clutching them to his chest. I picked him up, carried him to his room, and laid him on his bed. He was quiet now, unresisting, exhausted.

I chose one of his favorite stories, one that was full of the light of the moon, and of the stars—full of sleep. His breathing slowed and grew deep as the words washed over him.

I lay there listening to his breath, watching his peaceful face, his golden hair falling like down across his brow. I lay there for a long time, watching my sleeping son—afraid of what was within.

The Light of Day

We eventually found a preschool that would accept Ian. Margie was a new teacher, warm, kind, and accepting, just what Ian needed.

The years Ian spent with Margie come back to me in flashes of memory; happy pictures tinged by a growing fear that all was not well with our son.

I see him sitting in a small red plastic chair beside his classmates. The rest of the class is singing Christmas songs for their smiling parents. Ian sits there, a happy grin on his pudgy face, unable to sing along.

I arrive to pick Ian up. The kids are outside playing, a boisterous, roiling group chasing a ball around the yard. I smile, looking for my son among those glowing faces. Then I see him playing by himself under a tree.

And I see myself, standing there watching my son. I stand there knowing deep down inside that something is wrong, but I'm not yet ready to bring it out to the light of day.

{ 6 }

A Realization

It was late August. Michelle and I were a few weeks into the new school year. The contrast between the school year and summer vacation is funny; during summer vacation, days mean nothing. It takes the weekly arrival of the Sunday paper to remind me what day it is. Then, suddenly, the languid days of summer seem to fill overnight with the frenetic energy of prepping for school. I'm not good with change, and each year I'm pretty nervous facing a new class of kids. That year, I'd added teaching music to my schedule, and Michelle was pregnant with our second child, so I was really on edge.

Ian had spent the day with my parents. I was tired as I pulled into the carport of their house. As I walked the brick path to their front door, the lake glinted blue before me, winking a seductive eye and inviting me for a swim. Michelle wasn't due home for another hour— perhaps there was time.

I went into the house, and Ian burst from the back bedroom: his blanket, Jean, in one hand; Baby, his doll, in the other.

"Da!" he yelled, and jumped into my arms. Mom was behind him. She ran earth-stained fingers through her short hair. A bit of weed clung there tenaciously, green against a dusting of grey.

"Hey, Bug. How was your day?"

He didn't answer. He just wriggled free and ran back to the bedroom, from which drifted the sounds of one of his videos.

I turned to Mom.

"You've been gardening," I said plucking the weed from her hair. "How'd he do?"

"Well, it was a challenge today," Mom said in her diplomatic voice.

"What do you mean 'a challenge'? What happened?"

"He was a little wild, but we handled it."

"Come on, Mom, I need to know. What happened?"

Ian's tantrums had been getting worse, but he hadn't had a bad one with Mom and Dad before.

"I'm sure he's feeling the stress from you and Michelle . . . you two starting school."

"Mom . . . what happened?"

"He got angry when it was time to turn off his movie this morning. I couldn't catch him. Your dad finally got him, but he could barely hold him."

The words poured out in a rush.

"He was trying to bite."

"Your father couldn't hold him."

"He's getting too strong for us."

It was as though once started, she wanted to get it all out, to empty her mind of the frightening scene. I didn't need to hear the words. They were simply the fears I'd managed to keep buried deep inside, finally given voice.

"Once he calmed down, he was fine . . . he's been okay since, but it was a little frightening."

I barely heard the rest. Mom was being Mom, trying to make it all okay—but I knew it wasn't. I kept picturing Ian out of control, and my parents unable to restrain him.

I remember gathering Ian's stuff, making him apologize to Mom and Dad, and taking him out to the car. They stood together in the driveway as we drove off. I knew they were as worried as I was.

I talked to Ian as I drove, trying to make him understand how Mom and Dad must have felt and that now I was afraid to leave him there. I don't remember my words, but Ian began to cry. I wanted to cry too.

One image from that afternoon is still crystal clear in my mind. I had parked the car in our driveway, and Ian was sitting there in the backseat, pudgy little legs sticking out of his car seat. He was calming himself with his blanket and doll. His thumb was in his mouth, and he was rubbing his blanket against his face. His doll was in his arms, and he was clicking her eye open and shut with his finger. There was no other sound, just the click, click, click, of the doll's eye.

My mind went back to Mom and Dad, standing there in the driveway watching us go. I'd spent my whole life believing that my mom and dad could handle anything, but today Ian had pushed them to their limit. As I sat there looking at my son, a thought struck me cold.

If Mom and Dad can't handle him, how will I?

The Grocery Clerk

I was coming out of the staff room at school and almost ran into a small waif of a woman; a fragile teacup with gray wire for hair. She was a fellow teacher well down the road toward retirement.

"I've got a compliment for you."

"Oh yeah?" I said.

Maybe I'm finally making progress with some of these people, I thought hopefully. Maybe I'm finally fitting in.

I was something of an outsider when I first began teaching. I had new ideas and, I think, somewhat radical ways of going about them; radical at least to the teachers who had been working at my school for years and years. I don't think they appreciated this young upstart, and the woman I was speaking to was one of those.

"I was in Safeway yesterday," she said, "and you must have just left. The cashier asked if you taught at my school. She obviously knows you're a teacher."

My mind went back over the previous day. Michelle and I had brought Ian with us when we went grocery shopping, and he'd thrown a fit in the store. This wasn't just any fit; he'd pulled everything he could from his little two-year-old body, turning himself into a seething mass of rage.

"I'll take him out to the car 'til he settles down!" I said to Michelle over Ian's screams. His tantrums were becoming so common that dealing with them was becoming second nature.

"Thank God!" I believe Michelle answered. It was hard to hear over the yelling.

I tucked Ian under one arm and made for the door.

"This is so embarrassing," I muttered to myself.

Ian was kicking his legs now, and the screams had reached teeth-jarring intensity.

"Just watch . . . someone'll think I'm trying to kidnap him."

I felt as though every eye in the store was boring into the back of my head. I could imagine what they were thinking.

"Can't he control his own kid?"

"What a brat!"

"A kid like that shouldn't be allowed in the store."

I waded through the disapproval; my steps felt molasses slow. The door appeared before me with the hope of escape. As I passed the checkout stands, I saw one of the checkers whom I vaguely knew watching me. I smiled wanly (what appeared on my face was probably more of a sick grimace) and tried to act as though carrying a screaming, kicking banshee animal under one arm was not only a normal, but also an enjoyable pastime.

I made it to the car without being arrested, set Ian in his car seat, buckled it up (what a satisfying sound that "click" was!), and climbed into the driver's seat to weather the storm. It stopped almost immediately.

"You enjoyed that, didn't you?" I said to Ian.

Ian smiled back. *God, I think he probably did!* I thought.

"Let's go find Mommy," I said aloud.

"Momma!" Ian said happily.

I got him out of the car seat, put him up on my shoulders, and headed back into the store. The same checker was watching us when we came in. She smiled at me and seemed to be nodding her head.

The rest of the shopping went without incident, and I had pretty much forgotten the whole thing until the teacher at school approached me.

"What did the checker say?" I asked. *She must be talking about the woman who was watching Ian and me,* I thought to myself.

"Well, I guess your son had a temper tantrum."

"He's two," I said. We were trying to convince ourselves that his rages were simply a childhood phase, and the 'terrible two's' still seemed plausible.

"Yes, well, she was very impressed by the way you handled it."

That made me feel good. *I was embarrassed for nothing,* I thought.

"The checker saw you take him outside . . . she said how great it was. It only took you a couple of minutes, and when you came back in, he was wonderful. She said it was nice to see someone who isn't afraid to give their kid a good dose of discipline when they need it. I agreed with her . . . parents are too soft on their kids these days; a belt is what most of them need. We had quite a talk about you."

I felt sick to my stomach. These women thought I'd taken Ian out to the car to spank him, and worse, they approved.

"I took him out to the car to sit and calm down. I don't hit my son," I said.

The bell rang, and the conversation ended with that.

***

I often think about Ian, as challenging as he is, growing up in another home. He would most likely be one of the "walking wounded" I so often see at my school. It's hard not to look for "Ians" in the children I see everyday at work: kids who are regularly spanked, slapped, sworn at. Some of them walk around as though they are shell-shocked.

By a twist of fate, luck, God's intent, or what you will, Ian could have been one of those children. Instead he found us.

Hank Smith

The image is a frightening one. I see Ian just as he looks now, with his blonde hair and deep brown eyes. Indeed, those eyes are almost black. They are deep wells into which one can see all the way down to his soul. I see Ian, but he has been born into another family. Born into a life full of violence and fear. A life where screamed obscenities replace gentle words. A life where the back of a hand replaces a gentle touch. Where the whistle of a belt—splitting air and skin—replaces the sounds of a lullaby at night. I picture my beautiful son living with a family like that and having his future beaten out of him.

{ 8 }

Changes

I bought a children's book called Changes, about a boy who is soon to have a new sister. It seemed like a nice way to begin talking to my two-year-old son about Michelle's pregnancy.

I remember pulling Ian onto my lap, and as I enveloped myself in the familiar feel and scent of him, I thought, I am about to change his life forever.

We sat there for a while, and I couldn't bring myself to open the book.

"This is silly," I thought. "He'll be excited."

I pulled out another book, an old favorite, and read it to him. I let the familiar words wash over me. They felt good in my mouth, and I was comforted by them. Then I realized—

I'm not worried about Ian . . . I'm the one who's scared. What if the new baby has rages too?

I opened Changes and began to read. "On Thursday morning at a quarter past ten . . . "

And as we read, as we talked about the pictures and the budding life in Michelle's belly, my life began to change as well.

{ 9 }

And Then There Were Two

"**H**ank, it's time!" Michelle said urgently.

It was eleven-thirty, and we had planned a quiet Saturday evening at home. Ian was sound asleep, *Saturday Night Live* had just started, and we were attempting to snuggle on the couch. I say attempting since "snuggling" with Michelle in her ninth month of pregnancy was becoming a bit of a challenge.

"I'll call Mom and Dad," I said. *We're old pros at this now,* I thought.

I jumped up and headed for the phone, only to end up in a heap on the floor. Sebastian, one of our dogs, liked to run in front of me, trying to guess where I'm going . . . he never guessed right, and I was forever tripping over him. Cooter, his brother, made a dive for the pile. I looked up at Michelle through a sea of black and white fur. She was wincing in pain as she made her way to our bedroom and her suitcase.

"Hello?" Dad said sleepily.

"It's time. Can you guys come stay with Ian?" I think I was nearly shouting with excitement.

"We'll be right there."

I put Michelle's suitcase in the car. Michelle was pacing around the house.

"Do you want to lie down?" I asked.

"No . . . walking's better," she said through clenched teeth.

"Can I rub your back?"

"No . . . just let me walk."

There was nothing more to be done. The fifteen minutes it took my parents to arrive crept by; the ticking of the clock became unbearable.

Michelle is a "baby-birthing machine." They just sort of pop out of her in no time at all. By the time Mom and Dad arrived to stay with Ian, the contractions were coming fast. I loaded Michelle into the car and we flew through the warm September night to the hospital. Fortunately we were able to get her to a bed in the emergency room during the break between her last contraction and when she started to push. Kaylee was delivered by a nurse soon after midnight; the doctor arrived a half hour too late.

"She's so beautiful," the nurse said as she handed me my new daughter.

I wanted to say, "Yeah . . . she will be . . . eventually."

Instead I smiled and didn't say anything. New babies are ugly. There's no denying this basic fact. The poor things have just been squished through a ridiculously small space, and as a result they've been turned into an elongated, blotchy mess. I've seen a fair number of new babies in my forty-two years, my own two included, and it's always the same. Fortunately I've learned to hold my tongue.

I returned home at 3:00 a.m. and woke my parents. I vaguely remember sitting there on the end of my bed telling them about Kaylee, seeing their faces in the glow of the hall light: Mom's tousled hair, Dad's bristled cheeks. I walked them to the door and watched as they drove off into the darkness.

I was too agitated to sleep, so I wandered around the house. I stopped in what was going to be Kaylee's room. It was still not quite finished. I reached out to touch the bassinet.

Only two years ago, and Ian was sleeping here, I thought to myself.

I went into Ian's room and looked at his beautiful sleeping face. His long soft hair spread over his pillow like golden straw. I lay down beside him, his breath soft and warm on my cheek. As of this night, my heart was no longer Ian's alone. It now belonged to two.

"You've got a sister, Bug," I whispered. "You're a big brother now."

It's strange how a long-planned for event, a life-changing moment looked forward to with great anticipation and excitement, something dreamed of and longed for can also be so frighteningly bittersweet.

I spent a last few precious moments alone with my son.

{ 10 }

Perfect

I remember holding Ian in the hospital the day he was born. He was cocoon-wrapped and pink— with that milk breath smell—so new, and soon to become so familiar.

"Hi, Ian Bug," I said.

"Bug . . . where did that come from?" Michelle asked tiredly from the bed.

"I have no idea . . . but it fits."

And fit it did. To this day Ian is "Ian Bug," sometimes "Buggaboo," but mostly just "Bug" and it suits him perfectly.

Soon after Ian was born, we received a package in the mail from Marty and Jean, parents of my good friend Tom. Inside was a baby blanket that Jean had made. It was done in shades of spring, pale greens to yellows. We laid it next to our sleeping son, and it has been at his side ever since. It quickly had a name. "Where's Jean?" became a question frequently asked, sometimes in panic, at first by Michelle and I, and years later by Ian. The sound of his sweet voice, "Jean . . . Jean?" still fills my mind with memories of times long gone.

I don't know how long it took Jean to make the blanket, but I have an image of weeks spent sitting in the kitchen of that house filled with so many wonderful memories from my childhood. Jean sits there before the small fireplace, the crochet needles softly swishing. The old clock on the wall ticks woodenly, and the fire spits as a log shifts. She smiles as she holds up the blanket, admiring the weave.

The blanket is a well-loved shadow of its former self. Bits that have torn away have been tied back on at Ian's insistence; the careful rectangle has become more of a tattered snowflake. It is perfect.

When Kaylee was born, Michelle pulled out "Betsy Wetsy" from the back of a closet.

"What in God's name is that?" I asked, vaguely horrified.

What was left of the doll's hair stuck out at odd angles, and I swear the eyes held a slightly maniacal gleam.

"I've had her since I was six." Michelle sounded slightly offended. "And now that I've finally got a daughter, I'm giving it to her."

"It'll probably walk around the house while we sleep," I said.

I was rubbing away the pain from Michelle's punch to my shoulder when a three-year-old Ian toddled in.

"Da?" he asked, pointing at the doll.

"She's Betsy Wetsy. She was mine when I was a little girl," Michelle said.

It was love at first sight. Since that day Ian and "Special Baby" have been inseparable. Over the years, Special Baby has lost even more hair; she has maybe seven or eight strands jutting proudly forth. She's lost a finger, and her foot is bandaged to keep it from falling off. She looks like the survivor of some horrible chemical accident . . . and, she is perfect.

Words said in passing that stay forever; gifts casually given that become well-loved favorites. It's funny how things that seem insignificant at the time can turn out to be so important… so perfect.

{ 11 }

A New World

I pulled into Michelle's school parking lot as I had hundreds of times before. I tried to feel calm. I gave that up as soon as I stepped from the car and instead concentrated on trying to at least look calm. I walked around to Ian's door and unbuckled his car seat.

He's still a baby, he's not ready... I'm not ready, I thought as I took him by the hand and led him across the busy street.

"It's perfect. You don't start school until Wednesday, so you'll be able to take Ian on his first day," Michelle had said back in June when she saw my school calendar for the coming year.

It had sounded great then, with the whole summer still between me and that fateful day. Now I felt vaguely nauseated.

"He's in Jackie's class. He's known Jackie since birth. She's one of the best teachers I know. And Michelle will be teaching in the same room." Those words had become a mantra to me as the day approached. Today they held no comfort.

Suddenly we were standing in front of the door. "Welcome to Kindergarten!" read the sign.

"Ready, Bug?" I asked, trying to make my voice sound light.

"Yes, Daddy," he said.

I opened the door, and the colors and the noise poured out to greet us. This room that we had entered so many times before was now new and strange. Suddenly Ian wrapped his arms around my leg and we stood there on the threshold. I buried my hand in his golden hair. Time stood still.

Then to my relief, my joy—to my horror—I felt his hands drop away, felt those silken strands slip through my fingers, and watched as my son entered a new world.

{ 12 }

Homework

It was a beautiful evening. The leaves on the oaks were every shade of red and yellow imaginable, the air was crisp, and the lake caught the sunset and bent the colors into waves. Ian's first homework assignment was to take a walk and look for three things that reminded him of fall. It wasn't going well.

"Ian, look at those leaves, what do you see?"

"Huh? Leaves, Daddy, leaves."

"But do they look like fall leaves?"

"It's fall," he said.

"Yea, but are those fall leaves? Look at the colors," I said.

"Go home?"

He doesn't have any idea what I'm talking about, I thought.

I pictured other parents from Ian's class out walking with their children. I could almost hear their conversations. I tried a different tack.

I picked up a golden leaf and handed it to Ian. "Tell me about this leaf, Bug."

He looked at me blankly.

"Ian, what color is that leaf?"

"Yellow."

"Where did I find it? Was it still on the tree?"

Again that blank stare.

"It was on the ground, wasn't it? Why do you think it fell off the tree?"

He crushed the leaf to a fine golden powder and let it leak to the ground between his fingers.

"Go home now, Daddy... go home."

The sunset drifted from violent red to airbrushed blue. The leaves whispered and sighed; a dove called. We were silent now, but it was not a companionable silence. This silence was one of necessity—of circumstance—and as we walked on together into the beauty of that autumn evening winter began to creep into my soul.

{ 13 }

Us And Them

It was Open House and Ian's kindergarten year was coming to a close. Our anxiety over where to place him for first grade was growing as the end of the year approached. The realization that there really was something wrong with Ian was becoming increasingly difficult to ignore.

His expressive and receptive language skills were severely delayed; any sort of normal give and take conversation was impossible. His interests were so constrictingly narrow that he had no real friends in his class. He was an outsider, watching life go by from the sidelines.

His kindergarten placement could not have been more perfect. Basically he had three moms for teachers. Ian was in the morning class, and his teacher, Jackie, was a good family friend. Michelle was job-sharing with Anna, another family friend. They taught the afternoon class in the same room, helping Jackie out in the mornings. Ian was in the midst of three women who loved and understood him, in a classroom where he felt totally at home, since he had spent many hours there, literally since his birth.

But now it was time to move on. Michelle was busy with her class, so it was one of my jobs that evening at Open House to go to the first grade classrooms to try and get a feel for where Ian should be placed the following year. I brought Ian with me so he could see the classrooms and so I could see his reactions. I also wanted to see how the teachers interacted with him.

The evening was full of "Ian, put that down," and "No, Ian, you can't go outside without me." I'm sure Ian was picking up on the tension. He needed to get back to familiar surroundings, but I had one teacher to go.

Her room seemed rather plain, but she came right up to Ian.

"Hi, sweetheart! Are you ready for first grade next year?"

I liked the way she talked to Ian, and as it turned out, she was the one Michelle had in mind as well.

Ian was pulling things out of one of the kid's desks.

"Come here, Bug, that stuff doesn't belong to you," I said.

He yanked his arm away with a little smirk on his face.

"No!" he said.

Despite all of his language difficulties, he certainly had perfected a good, solid "No!" It was past time to get him out of there.

By the time we made it back to his classroom, he was starting a rage. Michelle was talking to a group of parents; she darted a worried look at us as I quickly took Ian into the office that the kindergarten teachers share, a small closet of a room in between two classrooms. There are doors with windows set in them at each end. I closed both of them and sat down on the floor with Ian in my lap. Sometimes I could stop one of his rages by singing to him, and by holding him in my lap I could keep him from knocking things over.

"Down in the meadow by an iddy biddy pool . . ." It was one of his favorites.

Ian was beginning to scream. I could tell this was going to be a bad one. *Should I try to take him to the car?* I thought as I rocked him back and forth.

Images of carrying a kicking and screaming boy through the parking lot made sitting there look a lot better. Michelle came in.

"Do you need any help?"

"No, I'm okay, just close the door."

It was funny how these rages had become so much a part of our lives . . . almost normal in a strange sort of way.

"Lived a little mother fish and her little fishies too . . ." I sang.

This was going to be one of those rages we just had to sit out. I continued to sing into his ear, rocking him gently, my arms firmly locked around him. It was then I happened to glance up. I was facing the door to the other classroom, and standing at the window were two women, probably parents of kids in the other class. I did my best to give them a smile, trying to let them know that I had things under control. I expected them to leave, but they didn't, they continued to stare. They looked fascinated, almost as if they were enjoying it. I tried to gesture with my head (I didn't dare let go of Ian to use my arms) for them to leave, but they just stood there. I tried to focus on Ian, but I could feel their eyes focused on the top of my head. I felt like we were on display . . . like animals in a circus.

"Step right up! See the raging animal boy! Be careful! Don't get too close!"

I wanted to stand up, scream at them and break out the window into their stupid little faces. But just as quickly as it had ignited, my rage died out and was replaced by a cold resignation. Every public interaction we had ever had, with anyone, anywhere, both the good and the bad could all be reduced to three words . . . us and them.

There are those of us who live this life . . . every moment of it . . . the joy and the pain, the fear and the hope—each and every day of our lives. And then there are those who never can really understand, even the beautiful few who try . . . us and them.

By now the women had moved on. Ian was calm now. The show was over; it was time for the next exhibit.

I half imagined their nose prints on the window.

{ 14 }

A Fight

"**D**amn you!" I yelled as I slammed my fists into the steering wheel. "Goddamn you!"

Michelle and I had had a screaming, mindless fight. I thought back over how it had started, but I couldn't remember. It was one of those fights where the words just poured from our mouths in undulating waves, each one meant to hurt, each one biting deeper than the one before—each one meaningless.

"You never can admit you're wrong," I'd said, "and I just take it. I'm the one who caves... I always give in. You walk around with that smug look..."

"You always throw that in my face!" she was quivering with rage, brown eyes flashing. I smiled inwardly, knowing that I'd found a soft spot.

"So it's all me . . . always me," I yelled. I tried to calm down, not wanting to wake the kids. "That's no way to have a relationship; it's supposed to be give and take. Well, I'm tired of giving!"

Like a coward, I stormed out.

I was driving fast, too fast, but it felt good. It was a beautiful night; the moon bathed the oaks in a watery light. I hardly noticed.

What if I slam into this tree? I thought. *She'd be sitting there waiting for me...*

My mind drifted into fantasy.

I lie on the gurney in the emergency room, breathing out my last breath. I can hear the nurse making the phone call.

"I'm afraid your husband has been in an accident. It's pretty bad, you need to get here right away."

She arrives just in time, gazes down at me with tear-filled eyes...

The images faded as I realized how ridiculous, how absurd the fantasy was. My anger died with the fantasy, and I turned the car for home.

The house was dark; she hadn't bothered to turn on the porch light. I fumbled with the keys, opened the door and went inside. The dogs were waiting for me, cold wet noses, nails clicking on the tiles. I made my way to our bedroom, stumbling over the dogs in the dark. I pictured Michelle lying there in our bed. I could almost feel her soft warm skin and smell the sweet scent of her hair. I stood with my hand on the doorknob, wanting to go to her, but I was afraid she'd still be angry. I couldn't face one of those nights where we each clung to our side of the bed, afraid to touch.

I went to tuck in the kids instead.

Kaylee was sprawled on her back, blankets kicked to one side, her hair spilled across the pillow in the moonlight. I pulled the blankets over her, stroked her hair, kissed her forehead, and went to Ian.

He lay on his side with his thumb in his mouth, Jean clutched next to his face. Baby lay on the pillow beside him. He looked beautiful and innocent, but as I stood there gazing at my son, I remembered that today he'd thrown a chair across the classroom. He was suspended for tomorrow . . . suspended, and he was only a month into first grade.

As I stood there watching him sleep, I realized Michelle and I hadn't even talked about his day. It was too much, too frightening, this violence that was living in our beautiful boy—too much for us to deal with, too much to accept. So we'd taken our fears out on each other.

Our room was silent, and dark; even the moonlight seemed afraid to enter. I climbed into a bed that suddenly seemed huge, too big for the two of us—this marriage bed and all it symbolized—this bed that had brought us Ian. I lay there on my side, feeling the emptiness that stretched between us. It was filled with the future. The unknown.

Michelle stirred, I felt her foot brush mine, and with that contact, the fears fled, and I pulled her close. Her warmth, her scent, and her softness engulfed me.

"I'm so sorry," we said at the same time.

At the other end of the house, Ian stirred in his sleep.

A Phone Call

I sat at my desk at school. It was lunch recess; the classroom was empty and quiet. The room was peaceful—I was not.

I slammed the phone down and swept the pile of papers from my desk in frustration.

"Hank, are you okay?" It was Jill, our school secretary, standing at my door.

How embarrassing! I thought. "Yeah, sorry . . . I'm okay."

"No, you're not. What's wrong?"

"I was talking to Michelle. It's Ian . . . he's having a really hard time at school."

"He'll be okay. You had both my kids in your class; you know how they were . . . all kids go through stuff like that."

"Yeah, you're right. I'm too sensitive," I said, knowing as I said it that she was wrong. This was something very different from what "all kids" go through.

No one at school knew what was going on with Ian except my close friend, Arden. I think in a way I was ashamed. I was also getting scared.

It was only October. Ian's first grade school year was barely underway, and already there were problems. Not just normal behavior problems, but major tantrums. He was sent to the office, screaming, two or three times a week. His behavior at home was deteriorating dramatically as well. The doubts that Michelle and I had carefully buried over the years with shovels full of "He's just immature," or "He's frustrated because of his speech problems," were being torn from the earth to be exposed in the brutal light of day.

"I hate this!" Michelle cried one day. "You don't know what it's like being there at school every day. I'm scared every time my door opens that it's Greg telling me he's got Ian in his office again."

"I'm sorry," I said, picturing Ian screaming in the principal's office. "It's hard for me too . . . I feel so separate from what's going on there... helpless. I just want to take him home . . . keep him home, hug him and tell him that it's going to be okay."

But we both knew that it wasn't going to be okay.

Things got worse as the year went on, and I worried that Ian would be kicked out of school. The teacher of the special day class was now helping Ian's teacher, giving her advice on how to handle him. It helped a little, but he was getting physical, frequently needing to be restrained.

"Here's how we do it at school," Patty, the special day teacher, said matter-of-factly. "If you can get him to a wall, you put your knee up between his legs so his feet can't touch the floor. Hold his arms over his head and wait till he calms down."

I felt sick to my stomach. Most parents sit and go over report cards at parent teacher conferences. We were being taught how to restrain our son.

"How do other kids react?" I asked.

Patty put her hand on my arm. "They're getting used to it . . . you guys need to remember that underneath all this, Ian is a wonderful little boy."

Michelle and I just looked at each other.

We'd tried everything we could think of . . . it was terrifying. We were both teachers, with years of experience working with challenging kids. I thought I'd seen everything, but Ian was different. As our frustration grew, so did a feeling of helplessness.

I'll never forget the phone call.

"Hank, you need to get on the bedroom phone."

Michelle had been talking on the telephone for quite awhile, and I could tell from the little I had overheard that it was about Ian. And that it was serious.

I walked into our bedroom. Ian was sitting there at the computer, playing a game. Brown eyes and furrowed brow, intent on the computer, he didn't look up. I reached for the phone.

Michelle heard me pick it up and said, "Hank, I've been talking to Laurie. The three of us need to talk about Ian."

Laurie was Ian's teacher. I think I knew what was coming. I could almost see her face, dark hair framing dark eyes, quick to smile; those eyes would be serious now.

"Hi, Hank. I'm not sure how to say this, but I need to tell you that I think we need to move Ian out of my class."

"It's really that bad," I said feebly, more statement than question.

"I can't control him . . . I don't know what to do with him anymore. I'm so sorry . . ."

There were more words. I suppose they were words meant to comfort, to assure us that things would be okay. They were empty—meaningless—and I don't really remember them. I felt for Laurie. I know how hard it was to have a difficult student disrupt your entire class. But what I remember most about that horrible evening was watching Ian at the computer as I talked, so absorbed that he couldn't hear a word I was saying. Ian sat there through the whole phone call, completely oblivious to this life-altering conversation taking place right beside him. He looked so innocent sitting there with his toothless grin, so innocent, and yet so out of control. I had absolutely no idea what to do next. I had never felt so utterly helpless.

When we finally hung up the phone, I wandered back out to the kitchen. Michelle was sitting at the counter; I stood behind her and buried my face in her hair.

"What do we do now?" I asked.

"Let's call Patty." Michelle sounded strong again. We're a pretty good team. It always seems that when one of us is weak, the other finds strength enough for the two of us.

Patty would become one of the magic people in Ian's life. At first I was horrified at the thought of her restraining Ian, but as I grew to know her, those feelings soon passed.

Patty spends her days performing miracles with those kids who all too easily slip through the cracks of the educational system; those kids whose physical or emotional needs are too much for the regular classroom. To look at her, one would never believe it. Red-haired and delicate, she fearlessly plunges into the fray, quick with a sharp word of discipline, quicker with a smile and a hug. Her classroom is a haven where children are treated with love and respect.

She was surprised by the phone call we'd received from Laurie.

"You know, he can't just be moved without all of us meeting . . . the principal too. We can probably keep him in her class."

"But I don't want him in a class where he isn't wanted," I said. "What do you think, Michelle?"

"Yeah, I agree," Michelle said on the other phone.

"We could move him to my class. He'd qualify with his speech delays. Think about it. It's a big decision, moving him out of a regular classroom."

"Are you sure you want to take him on?" I asked.

"I love Ian . . . I'd be happy to have him."

Simple words. Words that turned a huge decision into an easy one.

{ 16 }

Sticky Notes

A few weeks later, the scene was almost the same. Michelle on the kitchen phone, me in the bedroom.

"Hank, I've been watching Ian. I think he's autistic," Patty said.

"Autistic?" I said in disbelief. Images of kids rocking back and forth totally disconnected with the rest of the world filled my mind.

"But he responds to people," I said.

"There are lots of different types of autism, varying degrees. They call it the autistic spectrum, all the way from low to high functioning. I'm not sure exactly where Ian falls. There's one type called Asperger's Syndrome I sometimes wonder about."

My mind was reeling, trying to take it all in.

"You're serious?" I asked weakly. I felt scared as the word sunk into my head… autism.

"My son is autistic." Visions of institutions with urine-soaked, padded walls filled my mind as my anxieties took over, spinning away with that word. Autism.

"I'm sending home a book with Michelle tomorrow. Read it and see what you think."

We lay there together in bed, reading the pages that Patty had marked for us, her yellow sticky notes fluttering like flags. It all was coming together; this was our son—this was Ian. The words washed over me as, with each turn of the page, we took another step into Ian's world, and another step into the rest of our lives.

Thinking back on it now, I have an absurd image of backpacking trips high in the Sierras. Those yellow sticky notes remind me of the piles of weathered stones that marked our path. Like those stones, those bits of yellow paper guided us far from anywhere we'd ever been before.

Ian thrived in Patty's class. Within days, she had a huge support mechanism around Ian, from the yard duty teachers who knew exactly how to help him, to a teacher who took it upon herself to remind him each day as he passed her room not to run on the way to recess. Other kids even became involved.

I remember the day I picked Ian up early for a doctor's appointment. A girl I'd never seen before happened to be coming out of the library as we passed.

"How was your day, Ian?" She asked.

"Great!" Ian replied.

"Good job, Ian!" She cried.

"Who was that, Bug?" I asked.

"I don't know."

"Well, she sure seems to know you!"

With that phone call from Patty, we began our journey into Ian's world, for that is exactly what it has been— a journey. We had to make the journey into his world to find him and to really know him. During the past six years we've been holding Ian by the hand and walking with him. Sometimes we show him bits of our world, and sometimes he shows us pieces of his. This journey has been a learning experience for all of us, and it was Patty who taught us how to walk, guiding our steps with yellow sticky notes.

{ 17 }

Therapy

I remember the words because I can still hear them reverberating with their awful weight in that small, book-filled office.

"Your son has very severe receptive and expressive language delays. He hears what you say to him, the words go in, but he has no way of structuring or making sense of what you say. And then when he tries to speak, he has no way of retrieving the words he needs from his mind." The speech pathologist was a small woman, curly blonde hair, a serious face, and penetrating eyes. Those eyes were boring into mine now.

"So what do we do about it?" I asked feebly, taking Michelle's hand.

"Extensive therapy . . . lots of hard work for him, and for you two. Basically we're rewiring his brain and building pathways for him to express his thoughts. I'd need to see him twice a week for one-hour sessions."

My mind was numb. I felt Michelle's hand moist in my own.

God, it's an hour-and-a-half drive just to get over here, I thought.

"I wish I could tell you that insurance will cover it, but it's been my experience that they won't cover therapy related to autism. Here's a copy of my fee schedule."

We signed him up for Mondays and Wednesdays into eternity as far as we knew. We had absolutely no idea how to pay for it, or how to deal with a three-hour round-trip drive twice a week with winding mountain roads and commuter traffic on the way home.

This is too much, I thought.

It was early for dinner, but neither of us was ready for the drive home. My parents were giving Ian and Kaylee dinner, so there was no need to hurry. In my mind I could see Ian there, waiting with Grandma and Grandpa—my son and his autism; my parents and their hope that all would be well. I couldn't face any of them, not yet.

There was a restaurant just down the street, and soon Michelle and I were sitting across from each other, Ian's future on the table before us.

"I guess I shouldn't be surprised, but... ," Michelle looked exhausted.

"I don't think we wanted to believe it was this bad, but with the therapy..." I wanted to say, "With the therapy he'll get better," but the words wouldn't come because I wasn't sure they were true.

"Autism doesn't just 'go away.' He'll have it forever," I said to myself. The thought scared me, and I tried to banish the picture of Ian locked inside his own mind like a prisoner in a cell.

"The therapy is going to help. It's got to," I said aloud, trying hard to sound positive and strong.

"If we'd pursued this earlier . . . he's already six."

"We didn't. But we have now, and now we're going to get him some help. But we still have to be practical. How do we pay for it, and how the hell do we get him over here twice a week?"

"I can bring him Wednesdays, but there's no way I can do Mondays. I'm job sharing as it is, I can't just take another day off," Michelle said. "God, have you ever driven that road during commute? We'd be in the middle of it going home . . . two days a week."

I remembered my few times dealing with commuter traffic on that narrow mountain road. People drove like maniacs, flying blindly through the turns, all to shave perhaps five minutes from their drive.

"We don't have much choice. This kind of therapy doesn't exist in Lake County. We're lucky to find someone in Santa Rosa," I said. "Maybe I can leave school early on Mondays, or Mom and Dad might be able to take him. Maybe we can trade weeks, me one Monday, them the next. What about Kaylee?"

"Maybe your parents could watch her on Wednesdays. She's got preschool Mondays, so they're covered, but there'll be times when she'll have to go with us."

"God, it's even going to affect Kaylee," I muttered.

Michelle rubbed her eyes. "Let's go home. I'm too tired to think anymore. Will you drive?"

We walked slowly to the car through the first tentative drops of what looked to be a big storm.

Michelle fell asleep almost instantly, and I was left alone with my swirling thoughts.

"I can't deal with this," I muttered as I drove. "Ian having autism is enough . . . too much. And then we've still got to deal with all this mundane garbage . . . money, transportation, scheduling. If Mom and Dad can't help out, I don't know what we'll do."

It was raining harder now, glistening on the blacktop. Michelle stirred in her sleep and then settled again, her head warm on my lap, her breathing soft and even. Our car sped on through the night; inside we were dry and warm—safe from the wind and the rain outside. Michelle stirred again, muttered something in her sleep, a prayer perhaps . . . unanswered. I buried my hand into her thick, sweet-smelling hair and hung on.

{ 18 }

Building Blocks

"That's pretty much all of it," I said.

I sat across from Mom and Dad at their dining room table: Mom, her face shaped so like my own, so like Ian's, and Dad beside her, the black, bristle-like hair I remembered from childhood now going soft and white. They looked worried.

I'd told them about the visit to the doctor, about her recommendations, about the expense … I'd told them everything.

A picture that Ian had drawn was propped against a vase of dried flowers in the center of the table, and as I stared at it, my question hung in my throat. I was scared; everything depended on their answer.

"I need to ask you guys for something . . . we need your help."

"We'll do anything you need," Mom said immediately.

"Wait until you hear what I'm asking. It might be too much—please tell me if it is. Ian needs therapy twice a week, but it goes from 3:30 to 4:30. Michelle is off on Wednesdays. She can take him if you guys can pick Kaylee up from preschool and watch her until I finish with lessons."

"We can do that," Mom said.

"There's one more thing . . . is there a way you guys can take him every other Monday? I'm going to see if I can leave school early on the other Mondays."

"We'll do every Monday if you can't leave school that early," Dad said without hesitation. His blue eyes glinted. "Your mother and I can use the extra money for taxi service," he teased, laughing.

"I'll be following the buses out of the parking lot," I said. "The only problem would be kids whose parents are late, but I think I can get another teacher to watch them."

And what if my principal won't let me . . . what if I can't find a teacher who'll cover for me? I quickly banished those thoughts from my mind. "One thing at a time," I told myself.

It was getting late. Michelle and the kids would be home soon. There was dinner to see to and homework to go over; the mundane, boringly normal things in life. They were my anchor in the face of the gale.

Dad walked with me to my truck. The evening was filled with the sounds of the lake and the scent of rain.

I'm almost 40, and still coming to them for help, I thought as I drove down the long winding driveway.

I watched Dad in the rearview mirror as he closed their gate.

There's one block in place, I thought. *Tomorrow, I deal with school.*

***

I walked down the hall to the principal's office. His name was printed in bold white letters on a plaque hung above the door at the end. I felt like a kid again, slinking down a similar hallway towards a similar door to meet my fate. I was nervous then, and I was nervous now.

"Lyle, can I talk to you?" It was almost 5:00. I'd been waiting for a private moment all day, but every time I'd gone by his office, he'd been with someone.

"This sounds serious. You're never serious," he said jokingly. He looked up from a stack of papers on his desk, sharp eyes under thick grey hair.

When he saw the look on my face, he quit smiling and got up to close the door.

"What's wrong?"

Lyle was an easy guy to talk to, but today my words stumbled around each other awkwardly.

"My son Ian . . . he's been having problems. He just got diagnosed with autism."

Once begun, my sentences took on a life of their own, spilling over his sympathy. "I need to take him to therapy every other Monday. I'd need to leave right after school, but I'll make up the hours. I also need to start my private lessons right after school on Wednesdays to help pay for all of this, but I figure if I stay late on—"

"Hank."

I realized Lyle had been trying to break in for a while now. I took a breath.

"Don't worry. We'll cover for you. You concentrate on your son."

Three sentences, and another block settled into position.

I headed back to my room. Everyone had gone home for the day, and it was quiet... quiet as only a school can be when the kids are gone.

As I walked I thought, *Well, that's it. Everything's in place.*

But instead of feeling relieved, I felt depressed. I quickly gathered my things and headed for my truck.

"This is stupid. You should be glad that everything's worked out," I muttered to myself.

The tires sloshed through the puddles of yesterday's rain as I drove through the empty parking lot. I turned the radio on, hoping to drown out my disquiet with music.

My drive home took me past the local market, and as I sat there at the stop sign, I saw a family from school coming out. The two kids climbed into the car as their mom loaded the groceries into the back. A loaf of French bread was sticking out the top of one of the bags. She saw me and waved. I waved back and pulled onto the main road.

As I drove on towards home, I thought of them sitting around the dinner table later that evening. It was all so vivid…

Candlelight shone on the red of the pasta, on the glistening green salad, and on that rich brown loaf that had triggered it all. I could see it. I could smell it. I could even hear them as they laughed and talked, sharing their day as they ate. As the sounds of that family filled my imagination, the reason for my disquiet came slamming home. The images fled as fancy gave way to reality.

For us, for Ian, even the simple nightly ritual of talking about our day was impossible.

I turned off the radio, and as the silence settled into my truck, the bleakness of it all gripped me.

All the blocks are falling into place except one, I thought. *The last block will be learning to accept my son.*

{ 19 }

Toys and Washing Machines

I sat on the floor in Kaylee's room with the phone clutched tightly in my fist. I wanted to throw it out the window. Kaylee sat on the floor beside me stacking her wooden blocks into a tower and then knocking them down with a swipe of her hand. Over and over, the tower would rise from the primary-colored rubble, only to tumble to the floor. Those blocks mirrored my phone call.

I'd gone through a succession of insurance employees, my hopes getting higher and higher as each person passed me off to someone they were "sure would be able to help."

"So, you're denying us because my son has autism, is that right?"

"Yes sir, I'm afraid it is."

The only time I am ever called "sir," is when the news is really bad.

"But when we started this conversation, you said speech services were covered."

"I'm sorry, but that was before I understood that the reason for the services was autism."

"So, if my son had a stroke or brain injury or something like that, we'd be covered? Is that what you're saying?"

"Yes, sir," she said.

I could picture this woman sitting in a windowless cubicle somewhere breathing her air-conditioned, filtered air. She'd have a calendar with pictures of island holidays in the sun hanging from her wall, and pictures of her perfect son and generic husband would be arranged just so on the immaculate desktop. I could see her sitting there, safe and sheltered from desperate people like me hanging at the end of our phone lines.

"So, there's nothing you can do? Without insurance, I don't know how we'll pay for all this."

"No, sir, I'm afraid there's not."

I hung up the phone, my hopes crumbled with Kaylee's tower.

As I went to tell Michelle, I paused at the washing machine. Ian stood there on his footstool with the lid open. He was holding down the lid button so the machine still ran. He made a strange guttural sound, hypnotized by the swirling colors. I looked back at Kaylee singing to herself as she added stuffed animals to a house she'd just built. I stood there for a long time watching them.

Here was the enormity of what we faced, laid out before me on a bright Saturday morning. My children, quietly absorbed; Kaylee with her toys, and Ian with a washing machine.

{ 20 }

The Waiting Room

I sit here in the waiting room, listening to your screams of frustration coming through the wall. I picture your six-year-old body knotted in anger as you rage at the injustice of it all. There are so many words and thoughts inside your head, and you cannot get them out.

You come here twice a week and the doctor, an expert at teaching autistics to communicate, works slowly and calmly to cut a pathway between your thoughts and your mouth. She is building a bridge between your autistic world and ours. But sometimes, like today, the work is slow and hard, and your anger pours forth like a flood. I fear that the path, so patiently and carefully laid, will be washed away and that we will have to start again.

I sit here in the waiting room and I grip the arms of my chair to keep myself from running in to you. My fingers sink into the wood and leave their mark for next time.

{ 21 }

A Secret Out

"**D**o you have any questions?"

I reluctantly pulled my eyes from the view of Mount Tamalpais, and pulled my mind from the tree-lined trails with views of San Francisco back to reality, back to an autistic son. Michelle and I sat in a psychiatrist's office, where we'd gone for help with Ian's rages. Ian was in the corner, shooting baskets with a small basketball, using a garbage can for a basket.

Although this was a one-time visit, it had turned out to be one of the most helpful we'd had as yet. The psychiatrist wanted to be as prepared as possible, and along with all the usual medical reports, he'd asked for a video of Ian to be sent a few weeks before the appointment. The video was to include footage of Ian at as many different ages as possible, including a rage if we could get one. We'd put together what we jokingly called a "Best of Ian" video, complete with a bang-up rage at the end.

"How do we tell people he's autistic?" Michelle asked. "When he has a rage out in public, we've got to say something."

"Well, parents do different things, but you've got to be kind of tough-skinned about it. Just speak up and figure that the people who matter will accept it. The ones who don't, won't. I even know of people who've had cards printed up. One side says something about their kid being autistic and says that rages are normal. On the other side, it's got a phone number for them to call for more information about autism."

"I can't imagine just blurting it out," I said. "I'm shy enough as it is."

"Well, get used to it. You need to do it for your son."

The visit was over and as we gathered our stuff, my mind played around with the image of the "business" cards announcing to the world that my son was autistic.

"So, do you think you can do it?" Michelle asked as we drove home.

"Do what?"

"Just come out with it like that and tell a stranger that he's autistic."

"I don't know. Can you?"

"I don't know either. It just sounds so weird . . . artificial or something."

I didn't answer. *I'll never be able to do it,* I thought to myself.

"We could just do T-shirts," I said aloud. "Don't Mind Me . . . I'm Autistic."

***

Horrible screams, splintering doors, smashing toys, Michelle's sobs—the sounds of a rage poured out Ian's open window into the heat of the summer day, our shameful secret fouling the air. And when it was over, Michelle and I sat there in the aftermath, exhausted.

"Oh God, Hank. Look."

Michelle was pointing out Ian's window. Our neighbors were in their yard, working near the fence.

"Do you think they heard?"

"How could they not have?" I asked. "We've got to say something to them. It's summer, we can't leave our windows closed. They're going to start hearing us."

"We should've printed up cards." Michelle mumbled as we walked outside.

I don't know about Michelle, but I was nervous.

"Kathy?" Michelle called through the fence. "You guys must have heard Ian just now." She was trying to sound casual.

"He's autistic . . . he has these rages. They can be pretty awful," I said, the words felt thick on my tongue.

"I sort of figured," Kathy said. "I work with people with disabilities. A few of them have autism. If there's ever anything I can do . . . "

She went on, the words flowing into the summer air. I heard some of them, but mostly I let them roll past and instead marveled at how easy it had been. The secret was out, and the world went on.

***

I sat in the waiting room at the dentist and listened to the frustration building in the hygienist's voice as she tried to clean Ian's teeth. I could see Michelle standing in the doorway of the examination room; Ian flailing away beyond.

This was Ian's first full dentist appointment. Up until now he'd had quick examinations. We had both wanted to be in the room with him, but we hadn't been sure how to ask.

"You need to sit still!" the hygienist was sounding angry now.

I motioned for Michelle to come to me.

"Did you tell her he's autistic?"

"No, I don't know how to just come out and say it."

"Like we did with Kathy. We need to tell her. She's going to lose it with him."

I went to the door. "Can I talk to you for a sec?"

Her eyes flashed at me over her mask, but she put down her tools and came over.

"Ian's autistic," I said quietly.

"Well, no wonder!" she said, actually sounding relieved. "That explains everything. You should have told me at the start."

Her eyes were smiling as she went back to Ian.

"Let's try again, Ian. I promise this won't hurt . . . "

. . . and again, the world went on.

***

"GET OUT! GO!"

I screamed the words into the face of my beautiful daughter. She was standing there in the doorway, watching as I fought to pin her brother to the floor. Her eyes were huge and uncomprehending as she ran from the room. I wanted to go to her, but Michelle was gone, and I was alone with a son who had turned into a monster.

When it was over, when Ian had returned, I went to find Kaylee. She was in her room, lying on her bed, her stuffed animals surrounding her like a protective wall. She wasn't crying, but those eyes were still huge. I think that was worse.

"Oh, Baby Girl," I said, pulling her onto my lap. "I'm so sorry I yelled at you. I didn't want you to see Ian like that."

"What's wrong with him, Daddy?"

"Ian has something called autism. Sometimes he get's scary mad, like tonight, and Mommy and Daddy have to hold him down so he doesn't get hurt."

"It scared me."

"It sometimes scares me too."

And with those words, I guided Kaylee down the first few steps on the path that we will all walk for the rest of our lives. As I looked into those frightened eyes, as I held her close, I knew deep inside that this was something that I couldn't ever make better. As my words poured out into the quiet of her room . . . time the world shuddered to a stop.

{ 22 }

Teasing

I was sweeping the driveway. Ian was down the street playing with some of the neighborhood kids. This was one of those moments of letting go. I was allowing Ian to be off on his own and to practice his fledgling social skills. For most parents of a six-year-old, this would be no big deal, but for the parent of a six-year-old autistic, it's huge. I kept going down to the bottom of the driveway to check on him, and things seemed to be going okay.

We had been working hard with Ian on how to interact with other kids. Teaching him how to greet someone, how to make conversation; the give and take of a normal dialog with one's peers. These are skills that come naturally to most children through trial and error. For autistics, it is a real challenge and something that makes them stand out if it's not addressed.

"No, your name is Kevin," I heard Ian say.

"No it's not, I'm Steve."

"No, I'm Steve," another kid said. "You're Doug."

"His name is Kevin," Ian said. "He's my friend."

"No, he's John."

I was furious. I wonder now whether the parent of a "normal" child would react that way. I set aside my broom and headed down the street. The group of boys saw me coming and quieted quickly. I realized I was shaking. I wanted to scream at them, but I took a deep breath, and by the time I came up to them, I was in control.

"Come on, Ian, it's time to go home. These boys aren't being very nice."

Ian must have been feeling the same because he headed home without argument. I turned to the group.

"Do you guys know what autism is?"

"No," someone mumbled.

"He has a really hard time understanding everything that people say to him. It's kind of like all your words go into his brain and get jumbled around. That name garbage you were doing to him was really mean."

One kid stepped forward, the spokesman of the group.

"I just thought he had a speech problem," he said.

"So if he did, that would've made teasing him okay?" I asked.

I turned and headed back home. Ian was waiting for me on the driveway.

"Those boys were mean, huh . . . huh?"

"They weren't very nice," I said. "I'm glad you didn't get mad and yell."

"They were teasing me, huh?"

"Yeah, Ian, they were teasing you, but I was right there to help you."

We went into the house.

God how many times is this going to happen to him over the years, and I won't be there to help him, I thought.

This was a time when I just want the world to go away and to leave just us—alone and safe. It was then that I noticed the group of boys gathering at the bottom of our driveway.

"Great . . . what now?" I asked myself.

I walked out to them.

"Do you guys need something?" I asked.

The same boy stepped forward, spokesman again. "I just wanted to tell you that we're sorry. We didn't know. We won't do that again."

"What's your name?" I asked.

"Steve," he said.

"Well, Steve, you made my day."

***

Letting go is difficult for any parent. The steps down that road are hard: allowing a play date at someone else's house; placing the car keys into an anxiously waiting hand; turning an empty bedroom into a den. Our steps with Ian are smaller, and I don't know how far we'll go down that path with all its twists and turns. I always want to be there for him, there to brush away the dirt and kiss away the pain, but I know I can't. Letting him go is hard.

***

I pause in my work and stand there at the bottom of the driveway holding the broom. I watch Ian walk off down the street, so small and vulnerable. My grip tightens until my hands hurt.

{ 23 }

The Toy Store

Ian and I had gone to a toy store to pick up a gift for a family friend. Ian was around seven at the time. The store was quite crowded, hot and stuffy. As we walked down the aisle, Ian moved ahead of me, looking at the toys. I called for him to come back next to me; he turned, smiled, and kept walking.

"Ian, I need you back by me."

He smiled again and walked faster. He was at the end of the aisle now, and as I moved toward him, he disappeared up the next one. When I saw him next, he was at the end of that aisle waiting for me, but when I headed his way, he smiled and headed for the next row. When I moved to the other end of that row, he was at the opposite end smiling. As soon as he could see me, he moved on to the next one. I began to get scared.

"Ian, I need you here, NOW!" I said, desperation creeping into my voice. He just smiled and moved to the next row.

People were beginning to notice. I felt completely helpless. It seemed so loud and chaotic. Everywhere I turned, there was a crowd of people between us. I wanted to scream at the people in my way, standing between me and my son. I began to wonder what I'd do if I lost him in the crowd. He certainly wouldn't be able to communicate with anyone who tried to help him.

Maybe I should ask for help, I thought. The scenario played out in my mind. "Excuse me, can you help me? My son's gotten away from me." I could picture looks of disdain.

"He can't control his own son."

"That kid needs a good swat on the butt."

"I'd make that kid mind."

What if I told them he's autistic?

I could go up to someone and say, "Excuse me, my son is autistic, and he's gotten away from me. Can you help me catch him?"

That makes him sound like some sort of animal, I thought as I tried to sneak around behind him.

I was beginning to panic, *God, it's so hot in here!*

When I got to the next aisle, he wasn't there. I felt as though I would throw up. I went back to where I'd last seen him, and there he was looking at a toy truck. He was so absorbed in the truck that I was able to come up behind him and grab his arm.

I don't remember leaving the store. I buckled Ian into his car seat, locked his door, and climbed into the driver's seat. As we sat there in the parking lot, I began to talk to him. I tried to stay calm, but my voice rose and soon I was screaming—screaming out the noise and heat of the store. Screaming out my rage at those people in there with normal lives, normal kids, who could never understand. Screaming out my anger at Ian; screaming out the unfairness of Ian's autism. Then I began to cry.

It was very quiet, and it began to rain. The first drops hit the windshield with a soft hiss; the wind stirred the trees. The air felt cool and soft through the open window. I looked at Ian in his booster seat. He'd taken it all very calmly and was quietly gazing out his window at the rain.

I climbed into the backseat, kissing him, burying my face into the scent of his hair, breathing it in, breathing him in . . . my autistic son.

24

A Rage

We'd spent the weekend with Michelle's family and were packing up to go home. Ian was playing on Grandma's computer.

"Ian, five minutes" I said.

"NO!"

"Five minutes, then time for goodbyes." I ignored the outburst, but my fingers were crossed in my pocket.

"Please, no rage, not today of all days . . . not here," I said to myself.

I managed to get him out to the car, but as he was getting in, he bumped his head and the rage hit. Sometimes it's almost like watching him dissolve—almost like Ian melts away and leaves pure rage. It was like that now. He began to scream and run off towards the street. I ran after him and pulled him from the road. He was kicking, spitting, biting . . . an animal. Grandma and Grandpa stood in the doorway as I dragged him into the house. They'd never seen a big rage before; they looked frightened.

I took Ian to a back bedroom, called to Michelle for help, and settled in to ride out the storm. One would think that we'd get used to these rages. I suppose in a way we are, but there is something truly horrible about watching your child turn into a wild animal, screaming awful things, trying to hurt those he loves the most. You never get used to that. And sometimes, some terrifying, awful times, his rage soaks into me.

He is trying to bite my hand, and all I want to do is slam his head into the ground, to grind his anger out into the dust of the floor like one puts out a cigarette—grinding our rage into ash. I try to breathe, the sweat drips down my face, and I fight my rage as I fight his. I want to run out into the cold darkness, to let the air scream across my face and blow the rage away.

I hate this, I hate our lives, I hate the fear. I hate your autism . . . I hate you! You've taken all I have to give . . . I'm too tired to be your father . . . I'm done.

Thank God the words stay in my mind. The feelings are horrible, and they leave a taint in my mouth.

It was over as suddenly as it had started. Ian was looking into my eyes now, and I saw fear there, like he was afraid I would leave him. My rage melted away.

Sometimes I hate myself.

25

Ideas

We've taught you to breathe deep and to count to ten
as you let the breath go.
We've taught you to beat a pillow
instead of hitting us.
We've tried to teach you how your body feels
when you are losing control.

Sometimes it seems as if you have learned nothing.

And then at night, as I stand and look at the stars
that spill across the sky,
I ask myself,
"Where will we be, if we run out of ideas?"

{ 26 }

Soccer

"**G**O AWAY! LEAVE ME ALONE!"
The girl's screams cut through the noise on the playground. I was watching Kaylee play soccer, and I turned towards the sound.

God, I hope that's not Ian, I thought to myself.

Ian's game was over, and he'd begged me to let him go play on the playground.

"Okay, Bug, but you're going to be a nice, friendly boy, right?"

"Right!" he'd said confidently.

I scanned the climber where I'd last seen Ian, and there he was, standing next to a girl who was backing away from him—still yelling. To top it off, her parents were heading towards them.

"Great," I muttered as I ran over.

We'd only known about his autism for six months or so, and I was still getting used to telling people he was autistic when problems like this arose.

"Ian, what's going on?" I asked as the girl's parents came up.

"I was just playing!"

"Ian, she's really upset . . . what happened?"

"Can I talk to you a minute?" the girl's mother asked.

"Sure," I said walking over to her. "I'm really sorry if my son . . . "

"It's probably not your son." She looked uncomfortable.

Her husband came over and said, "She's got something called Attachment Disorder, and part of it is that she can't have strangers standing too close to her . . . her personal space they call it."

"Well, they make a great couple," I said laughing. "Ian is autistic, and he has no sense of personal space."

"We signed her up for soccer to work on it," the girl's mom said. She was laughing too. "It's been pretty hard on her."

We talked on for a bit. It was nice to talk to people who had similar issues with their child.

"I hope you keep on with soccer," I said. "It's been great for Ian."

Ian started playing soccer when he was in kindergarten. The socialization and discipline of working with a team has been good for him. He is good at defending the goal and is a genuine asset to his team, which is wonderful for his self-esteem. But as with everything in his life, Ian has taken the game of soccer and added his own personal flair.

We learned early on that it was a mistake to give any sort of compliment to Ian while he was playing.

"Great shot, Ian!"

"Way to go!"

"Nice steal!"

Ian would literally swell up with pride and stroll over to the sidelines to bask in the warmth of his fans. As the game roared on without him, he'd graciously nod his head to the accolades. Then he would slowly wander back to the game and the business at hand.

After much discussion before the games, we finally got him down to a happily shouted, "Thanks!" and perhaps a wave of the hand. No more trips to the sidelines.

My favorite memory was from his first year. Watching four and five-year-olds play soccer is a delight. The score means absolutely nothing as they happily clomp through the wet grass on their clumsy, cleated feet, black shorts hanging down well past their knees.

It was a cold fall morning. Michelle and I were standing on the sidelines stomping our feet in the damp grass, trying to keep warm. So far it had been a one-sided game, and the ball hadn't yet made it down to where Ian was guarding the goal. Suddenly a kid on the other team gave the ball a tremendous kick. It flew into the air in a cloud of grass and dew, heading towards Ian, who planted himself firmly in the way. But then something on the ground caught his eye, and he bent over to give it a closer look.

The sidelines erupted with howls. "Ian, watch the ball! It's coming to you!"

Ian responded by getting down on all fours, nose close to the grass.

"IAN look out!" His coach bawled at the top of her lungs.

The ball zoomed past Ian's face, followed closely by a sea of pudgy legs, all heading on to the goal. The shot was made, but the celebration was subdued as kids wandered over to where Ian was now lying on the ground. Soon, sight of Ian was blocked by the players of both teams, who all strained to see what he was looking at.

Michelle and I walked onto the field, and followed by the other parents, we joined the huddle. There on the grass was a gopher hole, its beady-eyed occupant looking out, wondering what the big deal was. Soon the gopher grew bored of these strange humans and returned to business underground. The crowd gradually drifted away and the game resumed, although not with the same energy. Eyes kept drifting to that hole in the ground, and the ball seemed to find its way to that side of the field more often than not.

Eight years later, parents still talk of that damp fall morning and the gopher that stole the day.

The rest of the kids from Ian's first team have moved on. I suppose one would say that they've matured. Today, a gopher on the field would be a nuisance, an obstacle to the seriousness of the game and the drive to score a goal and, ultimately, to win.

Ian isn't like that. He loves to get out there and play the game. He plays hard, but he genuinely does not care whether he wins.

Eight years later, he'd still stop and watch that gopher, and I'd stand proudly at his side.

{ 27 }

Awards

From the corner of my eye I could see Michelle gesturing to me, trying to get my attention. Her brown eyes flashed with anger. I was sitting at one side of the cafeteria with Ian's class; she was on the other with her kindergarten class. She was gesturing to the front where Greg, the principal, was giving out the last Perfect Attendance Award.

I knew what she was thinking. *They've forgotten Ian!*

She was frustrated, and with good reason. Ian's year had been a real challenge; he wasn't the kind of kid to win awards for good behavior. Perfect Attendance was something he could easily earn. It would give him the chance to stand up in front of his peers and at least be recognized for something.

The vice principal was talking now. I gestured to the front. I knew what was coming, and Michelle needed to watch.

***

"Hank, come here," Patty called as I walked onto campus. It was Open House, and Ian's second-grade year was coming to a close.

She was standing with Pam, the vice principal. Pam deals primarily with discipline, and unfortunately she had come to know Ian well. They looked excited as I came up to them.

"Ian is up for a year-end award!" Patty said.

"For what?" I asked.

"We want to give him 'Most Improved Student' for his behavior," Pam said. "We only give one kid in the whole school this award, and if Ian holds it together for the next month, we're giving it to him."

I couldn't believe it.

"Does Michelle know?"

"No, and don't tell her. It's been an emotional couple of years. We want to surprise her," Patty said.

"She's had such a hard time watching Ian go through this—having to be at the same school. It makes me feel awful when I have to tell her that Ian is in trouble. I want to see happy tears for a change," Pam said.

The next month seemed to crawl by. Each evening, I had to stop myself from rushing home to find out how Ian's day had gone. But as the last days of the school year dwindled away and our dreams of summer drifted tantalizingly closer, everything seemed to be falling into place.

***

Michelle was still looking at me, oblivious to what Pam was starting to say. I just kept pointing at Pam. Finally, Michelle began to listen.

" . . . and we only give this award to one student who has made the most improvement in one area. It could be anything, reading, or math. This year it is for behavior. I'd like Ian Smith to come up to the front please."

I urged Ian to get up. As I watched him make his way to the front, my mind went back to over a year ago and the phone call from Patty.

That call changed our lives, I thought as I remembered all Patty had done for my son. I looked for her and saw her standing off to the side; her eyes shining.

Ian had made it up to the front and was walking up to Pam. He gave her a big hug. Pam started to cry.

"Ian has made unbelievable progress with his behavior, but he couldn't have done it without help. When I call your name, please come up and join us."

One by one she called us: Patty, Michelle and I, the speech teacher, my parents, the yard duty teacher, even the teacher who helped Ian learn not to run out to recess. As we came to the front, Ian handed each of us a small sunflower.

"Why are you crying, Dad? Are you sad?" he asked as he handed me my flower.

"No, Ian, they're happy tears," I said. "I'm so proud of you."

I watched him as he walked on and handed a flower to my father. I looked around at the faces before me, each one also watched Ian; some were crying, some smiling, and all were proud—proud of Ian and proud of themselves. They had all taken it upon themselves to give Ian the gift of their time and energy, and there he stood, the result of their efforts, accepting his hard-earned award.

Later that day, someone hung up a picture of Ian in the teacher's room.

Under it they'd added a caption . . .

"Don't forget."

As I look back on it, a shadow hangs over that day, for I had no idea that the worst was still to come. That day was just the beginning of our journey. We still had then—we still have now—a long way to go. Sometimes we take huge steps forward, but often we slide back, for that is the way with autism. Those days are hard and frustrating. I gaze at that long slope before us with anger and, often, with fear. But during the dark times, I try thinking of that wonderful day in June. I think of the proud, supportive faces. And I think of those two words

Hank Smith

under my son's picture.

{ 28 }

In and Out

Before I wake Ian for the day, I always take a few minutes to kneel next to his bed. I lay my head on his chest as he sleeps and I doze for a few moments. I listen to his quiet breathing, in and out, like waves on the sand. For a moment everything is still and quiet, and my world centers on those gentle breaths
. . . in and out.

I remember when he was a baby, watching him as he slept. I used to feel for his breath with my hand, happy for those gentle puffs, wisps of air so soft, moist, and warm against my skin —smelling new, smelling of life—smelling of Ian. He must already have been autistic, although we had no inkling.

On the bad days, I sometimes feel as though the autism is separate from Ian, some "other" in his brain, hidden from us, yet lurking there with evil intent. It has no face and no name, but I know the damage it can do.

Those are the bad days, and I try not to let the fear grip me for long. Autism is part of who and what Ian is, as much a part of him as his fingers and his toes—as his beautiful, soft breath.

In and out. In and out. I let myself float away on the tide.

The Box

There is a hill behind my parents' house. Grey, green fields sigh in the breezes from the lake at its base; ancient oaks cover its crown. It is a point of land that thrusts out into the lake whose waters crash at its base. It is a beautiful, healing place where nothing ever changes. Near a rock outcropping that looks out over the cove where my parents live is a small stone. I placed it there during a dark time long ago and I visit it often. It remains exactly where I set it, surrounded by the mosses of twenty years.

Near the top of The Point is a beautiful oak. In my mind, I put all my worries in an imaginary box and bury it at the foot of the tree. I can dig it up and rummage through the box whenever I want, but the worries are put back and buried again when I'm through.

I've climbed that hill many times by the real light of day, and inside my mind as well. When I feel the need, I dig up my box. At times the box is overflowing, and at other times it is nearly empty— although it has never been completely empty.

At the bottom of that box is a worry that will never leave. No matter what I've added, or what I've removed, this worry remains:

What does the future hold for my son?

I examine that worry often. Unlike many of the others, it is real, immediate, and huge.

I hold it in my mind for a bit; then I bury the box once more and go stare at the lake for a while.

{ 30 }

Public Speaking

I was attending a two-day conference on autism at UC San Francisco. Perhaps fifty of us sat in a dim, windowless lecture hall in the basement. The class was open to parents and professionals, but I felt as though I was the only parent in the room. Everyone else appeared to be Special Ed teachers, speech pathologists, school psychologists, and the like . . . professionals who worked with autistics in the public schools.

The speaker was a nationally known expert on autism who was originally from Germany. She was an older woman, grey hair, intense eyes, and she was comfortably confident in front of the group. Many of the people in the room seemed to already know her. I felt like an outsider.

She had been talking about the challenges of working with autistic kids, but I was struck by the positive way she spoke of these challenging children. I'd never heard anyone talk about autistic kids that way before.

When she asked for comments, to my surprise I found my hand in the air. I normally hate to speak in front of groups, and when I speak of Ian, I tend to get quite emotional, which is pretty embarrassing. But here I was, about to give my perceptions on autism to an expert and a roomful of professionals. I thought better of my idea and quickly put my hand down, but the woman had eyes like a hawk, and she swooped in for the kill.

"You! You had your hand up. What did you want to say?" She said in her thick German accent.

"Uhh . . . yes . . . Uhhh, I."

The talons had closed around me, and I was dinner. I could either speak or look like a fool.

"My son is autistic. His name is Ian." *God, why did you tell them his name? I thought. They don't want to hear about personal stuff like that!*

Then I realized that this was exactly what they needed to hear; what this roomful of professionals *had* to hear. They needed to know about Ian's joys and his fears. They needed to know how he can spend an hour just dropping stones into the lake. They needed to know about his beautiful innocence and his rages, his obsessions and his gifts. They needed to know about his intense soul-baring brown eyes and how he wears his clothes inside-out because that way they are smoother against his skin. They needed to know what he liked at dinner, for God's sake—they needed to *know* Ian!

And so I began to talk. I don't remember everything I said, but I do remember the room growing very quiet, and my perception of Hawk Woman changing to that of a kind grandmother as I spoke. I could almost smell cookies.

I don't know how long I talked, but as I drew to a close, I could feel the tears in my eyes. My voice sounded thick, but for once I didn't care.

"I feel there is a beauty to Ian's autism and that with the challenges come wonderful gifts. If someone handed me a pill that would cure Ian's autism, I don't believe I'd give it to him because too much would be lost."

The evening's class ended soon after. As we filed from the room, I felt awkward.

Maybe I talked too long. What if I sounded like an idiot talking about beauty in such a devastating condition? Why did I have to say that about the pill? In the middle of a rage, I bet I'd give him a whole bottle.

No one spoke to me as we left, which only added to my anxiety.

The next morning, as I waited for the class to begin, a woman in front of me turned around and said, "What you said last night really made me think. My son is autistic, and I realized that when I think of him, all I picture are the awful tantrums he has."

A man sitting next to her said, "It's so easy to focus on the negative with the kids I work with. I really liked what you said."

Soon I found myself in a group of people all talking about their experiences with autistic kids, but I kept coming back to that woman. She seemed to need to talk about her son. It was almost as if she had always thought of her child as an autistic who was also her son, instead of her son who was autistic. A subtle difference perhaps, but one of huge consequence.

In the years since then, I've often thought about that woman . . . and I think about her son. I hope they've found one another.

{ 31 }

Words

When the day is done, after my final glimpse at the stars and before I head for my own bed, I go to Ian. There is a stone on his windowsill; a special stone from a sad, yet beautiful place in my life. It lays there next to his bed, as it has since the day Ian was born—smooth, grey, cool to the touch, unremarkable and yet full of meaning. I touch the stone, kiss my fingers, and gently touch Ian's sleeping head.

I tell him how much I love him, and last of all I say, "You're a good boy."

I say it very carefully and clearly so that the words will mix in with his dreams . . . so that no matter how his day has gone, those words will be a part of him.

Each morning as we head our separate ways, I say, "Be good. Have a fun day!"

These words are so different from those said at night. There is no stone, no ritual. They are just words I say, rote words, words said almost without thinking.

One morning, it was as though Ian had heard them for the first time, for he paused and said, "You be a good man today."

Those words struck me and were with me the whole day. They are with me still. I try to use them when my demons are with me, on those dark days when I fight them from one long minute to the next. The days when my demons find the light at the end of that long, long tunnel and try to put it out. When those days come, I don't feel like such a good man, I don't feel like much of a man at all.

But then I come home and I look at my son—walking the journey of his life—and his constant struggle to make sense of the world and to find his place in it. His words come to me.

"Be a good man."

I have so much to learn from him.

{ 32 }

Drifting

I feel as though you are drifting away,
A sprite on air.
Here, on this side . . . normal,
And all that is thought to be right and good.
And over there . . . autism,
Feared, shunned, and misunderstood.
But then I realize,
You were there all along . . . waiting,
And that it's me who is drifting,
Drifting towards acceptance.

{ 33 }

Conversations

"Daddy, tell me about Edith," Kaylee said.

"What? *Who*?"

Her blonde-haired head appeared in my rearview mirror as she leaned over in her car seat. We've spent a fair amount of time gazing at one another in the mirror.

"You know, Edith."

We were on our way to Ian's soccer game, Ian was absorbed in his Game Boy, and Kaylee chattered away as usual.

We've had some very interesting conversations on the way to soccer games. Unfortunately for our kids, the world has been an especially cruel and unstable place during their childhoods. They hear a lot on the radio. Ian is blissfully ignorant of the horrors of the world, but Kaylee asks a lot of questions. She and I have solved many a world crisis on the way to soccer.

"Who is Edith?" I asked.

I had no idea who she was talking about. In my mind I went over all the world leaders I'd ever heard of; the heads of the various terrorist networks; famous sports figures (I've heard of maybe two and I couldn't begin to tell you what sport they play). No one was named Edith.

"Tell me what you know about her," I said. "Maybe that will help me know who you're talking about."

"It's not a she, she's a he!" Kaylee sighed. Clearly this father of hers was useless.

I was completely baffled. A guy named Edith?

"Ian, do you know who she's talking about?"

"Huh?" was the muttered response. Clearly he'd be of no help.

"You know, he's that guy up in the sky," Kaylee said.

"Up in the sky? Is he some superhero?"

"No!" she laughed. "He's that guy who lives in the sky . . . on the clouds."

My head was swimming, "On the clouds? I'm sorry, I've got no idea who you're talking about."

"You know, he's the guy who got nailed!"

"Nailed?" finally the synapses fired. "Do you mean Jesus?"

"Yeah! That guy who got nailed!" she cried happily.

I'm not an especially religious person, so my kids have not been exposed to much in that vein. But mixing up the name Edith with Jesus? I explained what I could, and Kaylee seemed content with my limited knowledge. We lapsed into a companionable, yet pagan-like silence.

Driving home, I thought of our conversation and chuckled to myself. Talking with Kaylee can be such a delight. She'll chatter on and on, asking questions about anything and everything.

I'm talking religion with a kindergartner, I thought to myself.

I glanced in the rear-view mirror. It was quiet back there for once, both kids gazed out their windows in a quiet daze, watching the trees go by. I looked at Ian.

His autism makes communication in all its forms difficult. When he was in kindergarten, "conversation" consisted mainly of questions from us and one-word answers from him. The "Edith Talk" I'd just had with Kaylee would have been completely beyond him at her age.

Ian has been in intensive speech therapy since kindergarten. After nearly a year of traveling over the mountain twice a week for his appointments, Ian's school district finally hired someone we felt was qualified to deal with Ian's needs. Barry stepped quietly and confidently into our lives. A large, gentle man, he charmed Michelle with his patience, me with his love of Irish music, and Ian by making everything seem like a game.

Ian has made dramatic progress with communication. I remember the first time I had a real conversation with him. We were driving home from speech therapy, an hour-and-a-half drive over winding mountain roads; the price we pay for isolation and clean air. Ian was in first grade, and we had been taking him for intensive speech therapy twice a week for five or six months.

"Ian, do you remember when we got the flat tire?"

"Yeah, there." He pointed as we passed the spot.

He sat there on the seat next to me, little legs sticking straight out in front of him. He tapped the toes of his shoes together . . . tip, tip, tip.

"I was a good boy."

"You sure were! You stayed way off the road like Daddy told you to."

"And I didn't go by the car," he said. "Why couldn't I go by the car?"

We had been talking for quite a while, when suddenly I realized— we were *talking*. I wasn't just asking questions to drag information out. We were actually talking. Ian was telling me what he was thinking, what he was feeling, and though it was stilted and hard for him, I was finally getting the chance to really get to know my son. To actually hear, not guess, what was going on in his head. I was amazed.

A time came when I had the chance to publicly honor and thank Barry for all his work with Ian. His job was on the line; stupid school politics and huge egos threatened to remove one of the most important people in Ian's young life. There was an open session meeting, and I signed up to speak.

When Michelle and I walked into the room, I was shocked. The place was packed. At the head of the room was a long table where the moderators sat. They faced the crowd like a panel of judges. Given the choice between speaking in front of a large crowd and having a limb removed, I'd take the limb every time.

"I don't think I can do this," I said to Michelle.

"You'll be fine, just think about Ian," she said.

I was the third person called on to speak. I stood up, and to my relief, Michelle stood up beside me.

"My name is Hank Smith, and my son Ian sees a speech therapist in this district." We had been forbidden to mention the names of any person involved, or their school.

I felt the eyes of the room like drills.

"Ian has autism, and as a result he has severe expressive and receptive language delays."

I wanted to run. By God, with every fiber of my being, I wanted to run.

"Life with Ian is hard, but it was so much more difficult before he started working with his speech therapist."

My mind went back to the first few years . . . the rages, the frustration, and, most of all, the awful silence from a beautiful boy who could not communicate. My voice began to shake.

The rest of my "speech" was a battle. My tongue felt thick and lifeless as I fought to get my sentences out trying not to sound like a babbling idiot. My carefully written words blurred on the page.

And then I thought of that day driving home with Ian, and the first time I had really talked to my son. I thought of the two years since then; the joy of hearing the words and feelings that had been trapped in the whirling maelstrom in his brain pour out like a flood; they were released with the aid of this modest man sitting there in the front row, his job hanging in the balance.

Barry's back was to me as he sat there rigidly straight as though facing a firing squad. I pictured his warm, ruddy face. I heard his soft, gentle voice and saw again how patiently he worked with Ian, how well Ian responded. My last words came out strong and clear.

"It may sound kind of melodramatic, but he has given my family a real gift. He gave us the gift of getting to know our son."

I sat back down, exhausted, embarrassed . . . but also very thankful. Thankful to be able to go home that evening, prepare a meal, and sit down at the table and talk with, not at, my son.

***

Barry ended up keeping his job, but the petty politics of a small-town school district had soured him. He left a year later, leaving a hole in our lives that has yet to be filled.

"I miss Barry," Ian will say now and then. "Why did he leave?"

I've said it many times. Barry gave my son a great gift. What a bittersweet testament that Ian uses it to tell us how much he misses him.

{ 34 }

Articles

It's funny how Ian's autism has created a group of people at school who are on a perpetual autism watch. I'm kept very well informed by this dedicated group, and when I arrive at school, I am frequently greeted by a pile of articles torn from various newspapers that rustle in my staffroom mailbox like dry autumn leaves.

Some of the articles are a rehash of stuff I've read before. It's amazing how many ways writers find to say the same thing: autism is occurring in epidemic proportions, and no one really knows why.

Some are articles about the latest therapies—almost miracles by the sound of them. Those are hard to read. They make everything we're doing for Ian sound totally inadequate. We could almost become modern-day gypsies, moving from city to city in search of a cure, crusaders in search of the autistic grail. I try to let those doubts drift away.

There was an article waiting in my box the other day. I wish I'd never seen it, because the visions are stuck in my head and replay themselves in vivid detail.

An autistic boy was brought into a "store-front church" by his mother for a prayer session. Apparently the pastor of the church, in his infinite God-given wisdom, had decided that this boy was possessed by demons. They wrapped him in blankets, and over the next couple of hours, as the pastor screamed out to his God and the congregation responded with hearty "Amens," this poor young boy slowly smothered to death.

I can't shake the image of this child, wrapped up in a cocoon of blankets, almost like being in the womb again, warm and dark with the muffled sounds of the outside world drifting in. But this womb, this chrysalis, did not give life. It took life away. Did he know what was happening to him? Did he panic, fight, scream his throat out, only to give voice to the pastor's demons? Or did he die quietly to a background of muffled, muttered prayers?

But for a twist of fate, or perhaps God's will, he could have been Ian.

I think about God a lot. I'm not sure exactly what I believe. I do know that when I go out to look at the stars before bed, I am overwhelmed at the vastness of it all, the deep and quiet beauty. At times like that I feel that perhaps there could be something out there.

Some people speak of God as a mighty figure on a golden throne watching over us. If there really is a God, I prefer to think of him as an old man sitting on a bit of driftwood gazing out to sea. He is thinking about that poor child lying dead in a church, and he is crying.

{ 35 }

The Eye

This sounds terrible, but sometimes it's easy to take advantage of Ian's autism. School mornings in our house can be pretty intense, with all of us running around trying to get ready. I'm one of the worst, as I tend to sleep until the last possible second. By midyear I've got my sleep schedule so finely tuned that if I trip, I'm late.

Michelle and I were in our bathroom getting ready. Michelle had the hair dryer going, and we were discussing something when I noticed an eye at the crack of the door. I don't know how long he'd been there, but he was obviously telling us something, as I noticed a drone of sound (the actual words were lost to the hair dryer) coming through the crack. We were running late as usual, and we didn't have time to stop and talk. This can be a difficult situation, since Ian sometimes gets upset if we can't stop and listen to him. Much of what Ian likes to talk about can be pretty repetitive, so at times like this, it's easy to respond without really paying much attention. Ian usually doesn't seem to notice.

"Uh-huh," I said to the eye. That must have been an appropriate response, because the eye disappeared.

Michelle and I were talking again, the hair dryer humming away, when I noticed that the eye had reappeared.

"Oh yeah?" I said. Again I must have guessed correctly. The eye was gone for a couple of minutes.

"Huh? HUH!" Ian's "huhs" can cut through anything. The eye was back.

"Yes, Ian!" I said.

Right again! Three for three. Perhaps 30 seconds this time, and . . .

"Huh?"

He must have put all he had into this "huh," because it beat out the hair dryer and the sink, where I'd turned on the water to brush my teeth.

"Really?" I said to the eye, which promptly disappeared.

I began to feel a bit guilty, so I turned off the water and peeked out the door. Ian was standing in the middle of our bed, flailing his arms about. He then fell to the floor, rolling around with an imaginary God-knows-what. He was so into whatever it was he was doing, that he didn't notice me. I slipped back into the bathroom. Michelle was putting the hair dryer away.

"What was that all about?" she asked.

At that moment the eye appeared again, and this time we could hear what he was saying.

" . . . and then Tarzan fought the leopard and got him with his spear."

The eye was gone and this time it didn't return.

I turned to Michelle. She was smiling.

"I guess we just heard about the Tarzan movie," Michelle said.

"With the action," I added.

Ian had acted out a whole section of his favorite movie complete with a running commentary. Ian was appeased, and we hadn't heard or seen a thing.

{ 36 }

Violence

There have been so many rages over the years.
I try to accept them as part of your autism . . .
even when you hurt me.
But today, in one horrifying moment, all control lost . . .
I slapped you back.
God, if I could take anything back in my life, it would be that.
Today, you brought out the violence I never knew I had in me.

{ 37 }

Anger

With the right words, this rage could be avoided, but Michelle and I are tired. My anger takes over, and I can't find the words to turn the flood. As we have so often, we hold Ian down until his energy is spent. But this time our anger remains, and we turn it on one another. Michelle storms out of the room.

"This is what happens!" I say to him. "We're mad at you, and now we're mad at each other."

I put him to bed quickly, close the door, and throw myself into a chair.

What if these rages don't stop? I've asked myself this question many times before, and it always leaves me cold. *What happens when he's bigger than us? We won't be able to control him.*

The weight of the words I have left him with soon drives me back to the darkness of his room. I climb into his bed and pull him close. He strokes my arm with his hand, and no words are said for a long while.

Then . . . "I love you," he says quietly.

"I love you too."

Soon his breathing slows, becomes regular, and he sleeps. I lie there for a while longer, listening to his soft breath, and then I gently pull my arm from beneath his head.

He stirs. "I'm exhausted from that fit, huh?" he mumbles.

"Yeah, Bug, we all are. I love you."

"Love you too."

I go to find Michelle.

{ 38 }

Basketball

When fall changes to winter, Michelle and I pack up our folding chairs and move from the soccer field to a basketball court inside a hot, stuffy gym. Along each side of the long rectangle are rows of chairs, one side for the competing teams, the opposite side for the spectators. The scoreboard sits on a stage in between the two teams. Instead of the hideous buzzing sound of most scoreboards, this one plays the first six notes of Beethoven's "Fur Elise." We spend a lot of Saturday mornings sitting there watching Ian play basketball, and for many a Saturday afternoon, "Fur Elise" has become the soundtrack, going round and round in my head.

When Ian was quite young, he became obsessed with basketball. We had a Fisher-Price basketball hoop in his room, and he used to spend hours shooting baskets. He was very good; people used to be amazed. For a while there we had dreams of being supported in our old age by a basketball star. But then, as is the way with Ian's autism, his obsession shifted to something else, and his basketball hoop stood neglected in the corner.

One day he asked if he could play in our local kids' basketball league. We were surprised, since he hadn't shown any interest in basketball for a number of years, but we jumped at the chance to give him another social experience.

Sitting across the court from him has been interesting. During one game, he was sitting on the bench waiting for his turn to play. I looked at him and realized he'd stuck his hand down his shorts. He fumbled around in there for a bit while I squirmed in my seat. Then to my horror, the hand appeared out of the leg hole and it began fiddling with his knee. All I could think of was the line of parents there for the game—all sitting facing Ian. Frantically I tried to get his attention. When he finally noticed me, I gestured toward my crotch while shaking my head no. He looked at me with a rather puzzled expression, then waved to me. With the hand sticking out of his shorts.

I tried a different tack, repeatedly pulling my hand out of an imaginary pair of shorts. I hope it was my imagination that the family sitting to my left shifted away from me a bit. Ian, vastly entertained by my gyrations, winked and gave me a thumbs up sign. The other hand remained where it was. To my immense relief, "Fur Elise" began to play again, sounding the end of the quarter. Ian pulled his hand out of his shorts and joined his team in their huddle.

Then there was the time he scored a basket. We all roared with excitement, while Ian jumped up and down, waving his hands over his head. It was then that he noticed his shorts were untied. The game resumed, and the sea of players heading down court flowed around Ian as though he were some immense rock. He was momentarily lost to view. When he reappeared, he was standing in the same spot, engrossed with tying his shorts. Ian took his knot tying very seriously; his shoes were a maze of intricately tied knots that took days to remove. Obviously his shorts required at least the same devotion. He stood there alone, biting his tongue in concentration, creating the mother of all knots. Meanwhile, the ocean of players returned, and Ian was hidden again only to reappear as they headed down court once more. As he was nearing the end of at least the hundredth knot, the teams returned and he calmly rejoined play.

But the one I will remember most was during his first game. We'd never seen a game before, but it seemed to me that the referee was being hard on the kids; not mean really, just short and gruff with them, as though he didn't really want to be dealing with a bunch of ten-year-old basketball novices. Towards the end of the game Ian made a foul, and the referee blew the whistle to stop play. Ian obviously knew he'd done something wrong and was upset. The referee was trying to read Ian's number from the back of his shirt, but Ian kept turning around trying to say something to him. The referee was getting irritated at Ian and kept spinning him around to see the number, but Ian kept turning back, and I heard him trying to apologize for the foul. I don't think the referee knew what to make of this weird kid; he just wanted to get the game over with. But Ian was persistent, and finally he was able to make eye contact.

"I'm really sorry."

The referee stopped and looked at him as though seeing him for the first time. I cringed, expecting some harsh comment in return, but the man actually smiled.

"That's okay, it happens," he said. "What's your number?"

The game went on after that as before. I think Ian even made a basket. But what I remember most was that moment between Ian and the referee.

Many people have told me that getting to know Ian has changed them. I don't know if Ian changed that referee, but I'd like to think that he might look at what he does a little differently. I'd like to think that he chooses his words with a little more care and that he might look out for kids like Ian, kids who don't quite fit in with the normal sea of players he deals with everyday. Perhaps he might even be ready for the lessons those kids have to teach.

Among the many things I've learned from Ian is that you can't interact with an autistic as you would anyone else. There is no compromise; you adapt to them or you get nothing. That may sound harsh or cold, but for those who take the time, the rewards can be immense.

39

A Childhood

Some of my best conversations with my mom happen while I watch her cook dinner. My house, in its oak-filled hollow, is a short fifteen-minute drive from Mom and Dad's beautiful lakeside home. Living as close as we do, dinner at one another's house is a fairly frequent event, and when we are at Mom and Dad's, Mom and I usually end up in the kitchen as she finishes the last of the cooking.

The scene is always the same. An old jazz album, or perhaps a string quartet, plays in the background. The kids watch a movie in the bedroom, or perhaps putter down by the lake.

Michelle usually sits with Dad, talking or reading and drinking wine. And I'm there in the kitchen talking to Mom.

We discuss anything and everything. I'm lucky to have a mother I can talk to. She listens to my deepest and darkest fears and always seems to find the words to draw me back again. Lately, a lot of our conversations have been about Ian.

"You know," she said recently, "Ian reminds me a lot of you when you were young."

"Oh great, on top of all of my psychological garbage, I'm autistic?" I asked sarcastically.

She merely smiled and stirred the pasta.

I took a sip of wine and started thinking about the boy I was.

Although my childhood is now some thirty years in the past, I remember that child well. In many ways I'm that child still.

My life was ruled by routines, which at times bordered on obsessions. I had routines for everything.

I remember always walking to and from school the exact same way with certain routes for certain days. At bedtime, the same questions were asked of my very patient mother, always in the same order, with the same words, and always followed with, "Be expecting three calls." I was afraid to be the last one awake in the house, and I needed to know someone would answer when I called.

The anxieties came early, and at times in my life, they have been crippling. I hate myself sometimes always having to struggle towards the light. I look at people and wonder what it must be like to just allow yourself to feel happy and to not have a saboteur living there inside your mind.

Through the years, I have come to believe that along with my anxiety, as awful as it can be, comes a great gift. It is like a balance, and I cannot have one side without the other, the shadows and the light—the Yin and the Yang. As dark as my shadows get at times, the gift is always worth it.

It is this gift that draws the music from my fingers and these words from my head. It is the gift that brings sweet tears to my eyes and awe to my heart. It is the gift that allows me to see both sides of my son, for Ian is much like me; his autism has brought shadows, but it has brought magic as well.

Mom's face was lost in a cloud of steam as she drained the pasta.

"You turned out okay," she said.

Perhaps she's right, I thought. *I've got a good job which I do well. I have a beautiful wife and wonderful kids. We have a nice house. I'm learning to keep my demons at bay, and when I'm successful, I'm a happy person. Maybe Ian will be too.*

I think about that conversation often. On my dark days, Mom's words make me afraid and I think, *Maybe he got this from me.*

On my good days the words are the same, but I also add, *Thank God!*

40

A Bottle of Wine and a Good Book

Michelle and I were sitting in the living room, reading and sharing a bottle of wine. Kaylee and Ian played quietly in their rooms. It was one of those stolen moments; those times of peace made so much more perfect by the fact that they've come unexpectedly. We'd all arrived home at around the same time. Tired after a long day, Michelle and I decided to put dinner off a bit to give the kids some playtime and us a few minutes to relax before dinner. The dogs were sleeping at my feet, I was reading a wonderful book, we had candles burning . . . I sunk deeper into my chair. There is something wonderful about a companionable silence, sitting with someone you love with no need or desire to talk, yet knowing they are there.

Suddenly, out of the silence, Ian was yelling. Michelle and I went to him. He was frustrated by his video game, and it was escalating.

The rage is horrible. Ian leaves, replaced by white-hot heat, white-hot anger that has no beginning and no end. Anger that wells up from his soul and pours out like vomit—the stench, the heat—so intense. There is no one there to reason with, no one there to calm, so we hold him down and ride out the storm. It takes two of us now; two to hold him, to keep him safe, to keep us safe. He's drawing so much strength from the broiling emotion. His body is all corded python strength: fighting us, pushing, writhing. We are beginning to weaken, the rage taking everything we have, burning it all away. He's screaming now, horrible things, his voice like a chain saw. He screams his hatred for us, for life, for everything and the words fly like knives, strike at us, bite deep, and leave us bloody and raw. I think I hear a pounding at the door—the police, the social workers, attracted by the violence and the noise, there to take him away—the pounding fills my body. I find it is only my heart. My heart races away. The adrenaline pours through my veins. My head is on fire. We are being consumed, drowning in the heat, the sweat, the violence, and the noise. Trying so hard to be calm, to not add to the inferno by saying the wrong thing.

Then silence, but for Ian's heavy breath and Michelle's soft sobs. Ian is back, he is sorry and afraid. Kaylee is in her room; door shut. The rage has burned itself out, but the emotions remain for a while, floating and swaying in the air—anger and despair, but mostly fear—a fear of the future. You can almost see the emotions floating there, burnt and black, until they drift away like ashes on a breeze.

***

The house was quiet again, but there was no peace. Our books lay where we'd dropped them, and the wine sat in the bottle, forgotten.

41

Poppers

"**M**rs. Chase! *Mrs. Chase!*"

"Ian, she'll never hear you."

Ian and I were stopped at the top of the Ferris wheel. The county fair was spread out in all its cotton-candied glory beneath our feet, and there in the midst was Ian's teacher waiting in line far below.

"MRS. CHASE!"

Ian had put everything he had into that one; the car rocked gently.

"Look, she heard me!"

She did appear to be looking around. I could picture the poor woman down there hearing a strange voice drifting down to her from above.

The Ferris wheel jolted into motion once more, and soon we were on solid earth. Ian ran over to Mrs. Chase and gave her a hug. He's never been one of those kids who are shy when they see their teacher out in public.

"Did you hear me, I was calling from up there, you heard me, huh?"

"Well, I thought I was hearing something," she said.

She looked genuinely glad to see Ian and quickly introduced him to her family. The school year had just begun. Ian had been in her class only a few weeks, but he had settled in happily enough. It had been a difficult decision, a choice between a regular classroom and a return to the Special Day program. Ian had been working very successfully in a regular class for the past two years, and the school's psychologist saw it as a step backwards to go into the Special Day class again. Funny that such an important decision, and as it turned out, one of the best we've ever made was based largely on Alka Seltzer.

***

"You're Ian's Dad, right? I'm Laurie . . . Laurie Chase."

She got up from a table where she'd been working with a boy. An aide immediately took her place. Laurie was a new teacher at the school, still working on her Special Ed Credential, but teaching on a waiver. She came over to me and extended a hand; medium height, tousled hair, bright eyes, I felt instantly at ease.

I was observing classes to decide where to place Ian for fourth grade. I hated this job, since I always felt like an intruder. I would quietly sneak into the classrooms and try to look as friendly and unthreatening as possible so the poor teacher on display didn't feel uncomfortable. It's kind of strange that I would feel this way, because in my own classroom I have parents in and out all the time at the end of the year, and I could care less.

"Want me to show you around?"

"Sure. I'm not interrupting am I?" I asked.

"Oh, it's fine. My aides will cover for me."

I looked around. There were maybe twelve kids in the room, spanning three or four grade levels, two aides, and near silence, but not that dreadful, fear-filled silence from some of the tyrannical classrooms of my childhood. This was a comfortable silence, relaxed and peaceful.

Laurie led me around the room showing me the various stations she had set up: math, language arts, science.

"Each kid has their own program that we set up. They work along as slowly or as quickly as they want. The trick is to make sure they are always challenged. Luckily I've got lots of help, so my kids get lots of one-on-one attention. I'm still learning though, and—"

I thought back on the fourth grade class I'd just seen. When I walked in, I had been struck by a sea of bodies—over thirty kids were crammed into the small portable classroom—but the teacher had been great, exuberant and exciting. The walls were covered with wonderful samples of the year's work. The kids were engaged and excitedly called out answers. Then I noticed a boy in the back of the room, his book was open and he looked as though he was paying attention, but something about him drew me closer. I quietly moved behind him and saw that he was on the wrong page.

That would be Ian, I thought.

"You've got to see this!" Laurie's voice brought me back. She was holding a plastic film canister. "Take it."

"What is it?" I asked. The kids were smiling as they watched us.

"We call them Poppers . . . just wait a minute."

As she said it, there was a loud *POP*! and the lid flew off into the air.

"Isn't that great!" Laurie was smiling delightedly. "A little water, an Alka Seltzer tablet, and pop on the lid . . . I use it for a reward when my kids get their work done."

I knew then that this was where I wanted Ian to be.

People have asked me why we moved Ian back into the Special Day class. I tell them of Laurie's infinite patience and love for my son. I tell them of the quiet calm of that classroom. I tell them how Ian has discovered a love of math and how he is the acknowledged "Math King." I tell them how easily and comfortably Ian fits in; how under Laurie's careful and patient guidance he has thrived. I tell them that, looking back over the past two years, I know it's one of the best decisions we've ever made. I just avoid mentioning the Alka Seltzer.

{ 42 }

Innocence

"Daddy, you love Ian more than me," Kaylee said in her "Petulant Baby Voice" that I have come to hate so well.

Yes, I hate that voice, and the child in me could easily have responded with, "Yep, you better believe it! I've always loved Ian more and I always will!"

Fortunately for us all, "Daddy" answered instead. "Don't be silly, you know that's not true."

Not to be left out of the act, "Teacher" chimed in with a trite, "I'd hear you better if you'd use your nine-year-old voice, not your two-year-old voice."

That challenge has been thrown at me, as I'm sure it is thrown at all fathers with more than one child, since the day she learned to talk. Usually I let it go with a few stock words of reassurance that have become so automatic I'm barely conscious of them anymore. For some reason though, this time was different.

When "Petulant Baby Voice" was gone, I went to her. She was in her room playing on the floor with her stuffed animals.

"Kaylee, do you really think I love Ian more than you?" I asked.

"No, Dad. I was mad."

"You understand that sometimes Ian takes a lot of Mommy and

Daddy's time."

"Yeah, 'cuz of his autism."

"Yes, because of his autism," I said. "But even though it seems like we spend more time with him, it doesn't mean we love him more. We're just working hard to help him learn to control his autism. Are you okay?"

"Yeah," she said.

I reached out and pushed her over backwards.

"Are you sure?"

"Yeah, Daddy." She laughed.

Kaylee is a beautiful little girl—fourth grade already—but always my little girl. Kaylee (kayleigh) is an Irish word meaning party. Perfect for my daughter. One looks at her and sees brightness, laughter, and joyful exuberance. She is gentle, caring, and kind and so good with Ian.

I often think about the future when Michelle and I are no longer here. I think about Ian without us and am so grateful that he will have Kaylee—and that Kaylee will have him.

"And I had to talk you into having her!" Michelle will often say to me.

It was one of those nights. It was bedtime, Ian was on the edge of a rage and Michelle was on the edge of tears. It really doesn't matter what it was about . . . just the same emotions cloaked in different words.

"I'll go in to him," I said to her. "Maybe a different voice will help."

Michelle just pushed past me, crying now, and headed for the living room. I moved to Ian's door, steeling myself as I reached to open it.

"I can't do this yet," I said to myself.

Turning aside, I went to Kaylee's room.

She was snuggled up in bed reading; her bedside lamp cast a warm glow on her face. A jungle of stuffed animals surrounded her . . . her special blankets arranged just so. I sat down on her bed. She was completely lost in her book and didn't look up, so I said nothing.

As she read, she whispered the words to herself, the sounds of leaves rustling in a gentle breeze. Her words sounded almost like muttered prayer, and to me on this awful night, they were. I sat there listening and looking around the room. Here was peace, and here was quiet. Here was innocence and normality . . . plain, simple, and infinitely comforting.

Toys lay strewn at my feet, among them were small plastic figures in a house of blocks. I found the mother, the father, and two children. It was beautiful in its calm simplicity; a meal was laid on the table, and the beds were ready for the night. This was Kaylee's imaginary world where there were no screams of rage and where the mother had no need for tears.

I sat there listening to her rustling words and watched her beautiful face. I sat there and I basked in her normality, let it soak into my skin and smooth out the jagged edges of that night. I sat there for a long time, and when I was strong again I rose, kissed a silent thank you on her brow, and went to Ian.

It has been said that one finds strength in strange places. I find it often in the sweet innocence of my beautiful daughter.

{ 43 }

The Summer of the Tooth

The summer of 2003 has gone down in the annals of my family as "The Summer of the Tooth. Ian had a strange tooth growing sideways in the gum behind his two front teeth. It needed to come out, and that July seemed the perfect time to do it. We had a trip to San Diego planned for the last two weeks of the month, but the oral surgeon assured us that Ian would be fine by then.

At first Ian seemed very nonchalant about the whole thing, but as the day grew closer, he began asking questions.

"Will I be asleep like for my ears?"

Ian had had tubes put in his ears twice and was under general anesthetic both times. Watching my six-year-old autistic son get stoned on the anesthetic was hysterical. Half of me wanted to put on some Pink Floyd and join him in his reverie.

"No, Ian. They are going to give you some medicine that you breathe. It will make you feel kind of silly and sleepy, but you won't be asleep."

He looked distressed. "Oh no, it's gonna hurt!"

"No, Ian. You'll be too relaxed and happy. I'll see if I can be in there with you." He didn't look convinced.

The night before the surgery, the doctor's office called to make sure we didn't have any questions.

"He's seeming pretty worried," I said. "Is there any way I can be in the room with him?"

Over the years I've been "in the room" with him fairly often, from a hermetically sealed chamber for a brain scan to the x-ray room at the dentist. Because of my son, I've had so many doses of x-rays that I'm sure I must glow softly at night; hopefully it's a pretty sight.

"Oh, no!" the woman sounded surprised. "We never allow parents in with their children. It's far too traumatic!"

"You know he's autistic right? It calms him to have me there."

"You can be in the room until the doctor starts the procedure," she said. "And then you'll have to wait outside."

I broke the news to Ian.

"I'll be in there as long as I can, but then they said I have to leave. You'll be fine."

"It's gonna hurt," he said.

We had a ninety-minute drive to the doctor's office. We were to give Ian a half-dose of Valium a half an hour before the surgery to help him relax. As far as I could tell, it had absolutely no effect. Ian was pretty scared when we got there.

Fortunately there was no waiting; they were ready for us when we arrived. Michelle stayed in the lobby with Kaylee.

The nurse helped Ian into the chair.

"Didn't you give him the Valium?" she asked me as Ian lay there stiff as a board.

"A half-hour ago like you guys said."

She turned on the laughing gas, but she didn't look very confident.

The doctor came in and quickly went over the procedure with Ian again.

" First, I'm going to have you breathe this funny-smelling gas. It'll make you feel sleepy. Then I'm going to give you a couple of shots in your gum."

"It's going to hurt!" Ian wailed.

"No, no . . . they'll be quick little pricks, then they'll be done.

Besides, you'll feel relaxed and sleepy from the gas." He turned to me. "You did give him the Valium?"

I nodded. He glanced quickly at the nurse. I think we were all getting nervous.

The gas went fine. Ian was laughing and relaxed, but when he saw the needle he began to moan. I put my head right by his ear.

"You'll be fine, Bug."

With the first shot he began to scream. I'm sure the hair on my arms was standing on end. The sound was like a million fingers being dragged slowly down an endless chalkboard. I could only imagine the poor patients waiting their turn in the lobby, their eyes wide as they heard his banshee howl.

By the last shot, I was lying on top of him, holding him down. There were words now, mixed with the screams.

"Dad, you lied! It hurts!"

It broke my heart.

The doctor was well into the extraction process when I realized I wasn't supposed to be in the room.

"Shouldn't I leave?" I whispered to the nurse.

She looked panicked at the thought and quickly shook her head no.

And then it was over. The stitches were in; a kind that dissolved on their own. The doctor said it would save us a trip in to have them removed. I wondered whether he just didn't want to see us again. Ian was happy, all was forgiven. We headed home, exhausted.

We had just walked in the door when Ian said, "Hey Dad, what's this?"

To my horror I saw a bit of string dangling from his hand. It was one of the stitches.

I quickly got on the phone to the doctor.

"He's taken out one of the stitches!"

"He must be playing with them with his tongue. I put in four . . .

he'll be okay with three. Tell him he's got to leave them alone."

Telling Ian not to mess with something that feels strange to him is useless. When he has a loose tooth, he literally drives everyone around him mad until he finally gets it out. An hour later another stitch was out.

"He should be okay with two . . . one, well maybe. Call me if he takes another out."

"Ian, we're going to have to go back and do it all again if you don't leave the stitches alone!" I told him in desperation.

"It'll hurt!" he wailed.

"THEN LEAVE THEM ALONE!"

We were back in the chair the next day. They'd scheduled us for lunch time when the place would be empty; I'm sure so another set of waiting patients wouldn't be terrified of dentists for the rest of their lives.

It went pretty much like the day before. The only change was the whole dose of Valium on the way and at least half a tank of gas during the procedure—neither of which made the slightest difference. This time the doctor put in non-dissolving stitches.

"He'll never get these out," he said.

Ian had the first one out before we got home.

The rest of the month was spent trying to keep the wound closed. Ian managed to get the last stitch out three days later, and as a result he ate nothing but applesauce, yogurt, Jell-O, and pudding for weeks. We canceled the trip to San Diego.

I sometimes wonder if they have the same policy at that dentist's office.

"Hi, this is your dentist calling. We have your child down for an extraction tomorrow. Is he by any chance autistic? Oh, he is. In that case would you please triple the Valium dose, plan on staying in the operating room with him, and would you mind terribly coming at lunch time?"

As awful as the experience was, I do have one wonderful memory.

Ian and I are lying on the hide-a-bed in the family room. It is the night after the second set of stitches and I am trying to put him to sleep. Ian is truly traumatized, obsessed with the stitches in his mouth . . . fighting to keep his tongue away . . . terrified that he'll have to go back for a third time.

We have his lullaby tape on. Ian has gone to sleep to this music nearly every night of his life from the day we brought him home. The windows are open to the soft, summer scented night air, to the sounds of the crickets . . . to the summer stars. Ian is snuggled by my side. My hand strokes his hair; he smells good. His breathing slows and becomes regular and deep.

I think to myself, *How many fathers can still cuddle with their ten-year-old sons, comfort them . . . and take away the fear and pain?*

That quiet, gentle night is one of the gifts of autism.

{ 44 }

Halloween

Halloween is a major event on Ian's social calendar. He puts incredible effort into the choosing of a costume. Planning for the next year literally begins the day after Halloween. This has become tradition on the next day at breakfast.

"Dad, Halloween is over."

"Yes, Ian, Halloween is over."

"It was last night, huh?"

"Yep! Now we can look forward to Thanksgiving and Christmas . . . to winter."

"It will be a whole year till next Halloween, huh?"

"You're right, next October."

"Next year I'm going to be a . . ."

It could be anything. One year he wanted to be a hole. God only knows where he came up with that one. I thought it sounded great, certainly creative. Michelle, the resident Halloween costume maker, wasn't nearly as excited. By spring, he'd changed his mind and decided to be fire instead. Again I thought it was a fine idea. Michelle just shook her head. I believe that year he settled on being one of the 101 Dalmatians. Michelle jumped on that idea, a white sweat suit with black spots. Ian looked great.

Last year he was a pirate. On Halloween, the kids at Ian and Kaylee's school always came dressed up in their costumes for parties and a parade. We were getting ready for the big day. Breakfast was finished and we were gathering the last bits of their costumes.

"Where's my eye patch?"

"Where did you leave it?" Michelle asked.

"I didn't leave it anywhere!" Ian was sounding upset.

We were really running late. Michelle and I were both stressed; we both were facing Halloween with our respective kindergarten classes. Halloween in kindergarten is a special kind of Hell that only a fellow teacher can truly appreciate.

"Let's look in your room," I said. The eye patch was nowhere to be found.

"God, the last thing we need is a rage!" I muttered to myself.

"Why don't you and Kaylee head to the car. Mommy and I will look for your eye patch."

"I have to have my eye patch! I'm not Captain Hook without my eye patch!" Ian was beginning to lose it.

"Just head to the car. Mommy and I will look," I said.

We tore the house apart . . . literally. The thought of dealing with a rage, today of all days, lent a certain "edge" to the search.

"We've got to find it! He's planned this costume all year. He's going to go crazy!" Michelle said.

"I know . . . God, if he has a fit, it will set off his whole day." With all the excitement of Halloween, I didn't think Ian could handle the rest of the day if things went wrong now.

We never did find the eye patch. Michelle was crying in frustration.

"I'll go talk to him." I said. "Try and calm down."

"You don't have to drive to work with him throwing a fit!" she said.

I went out to the car. Ian was sitting there looking at a book. I opened his door.

"Ian," I said, trying to sound as calm as possible while steeling myself for his rage. He looked up.

"Did you find it?"

"Ian, I need you to try to be as calm as you can."

"But did you find it?"

Cringing inwardly I said, "No, we didn't." The key here was to keep talking, quickly and calmly. "We couldn't find it anywhere, so you won't have it for today, but we'll get another at the store, so your costume will be fine for tonight."

"I think it would be hard to walk around with an eye patch on all day anyway," I added lamely. I braced myself for the storm.

"Okay," he said, and went back to his book.

I stood there for a moment in stunned silence and then walked back into the house in a daze. Michelle was putting her shoes on, still crying.

"What did he say?" she asked.

"He said okay."

"That's it . . . that's all he said . . . 'okay'?"

Michelle and I looked around at our house. It was in shambles after our frantic search; we began to laugh.

Because we live in the country, it takes us about an hour to trick or treat around our "block." There aren't many houses and not everyone encourages trick-or-treaters, but we have to stop in front of each house and discuss it.

"Can we go to this house, Dad?"

"Well, look at the front door, do they have any lights on?"

"They don't want any trick-or-treaters, huh, Dad, huh?"

"No, it doesn't look like it," I say, and so we move on.

"What about this house . . . huh? . . . this house?"

"There's a pumpkin out front; what do you think?"

"The light's on . . . we can go, huh?"

"Remember to say thank you."

At first, he used to walk right on in when people would answer the door, usually reciting a dissertation of his year's quest for the perfect Halloween costume. I remember a little old lady in particular who had to jump out of the way as Ian leaped through her door.

"Trick-or-treat! I was going to be a hole, but then I wanted to be fire, but I'm 101 Dalmatians. I like 101 Dalmatians. Have you seen 101 Dalmatians? Horace and Jasper got stuck on the fence . . . !"

She was filling his bag, rather frantically I thought, trying to appease him with candy and ease him out the door at the same time.

"THANK YOU!" he yelled. "I like your pumpkin. Mine is a scary face and a sad face, and a mad face . . . " (Ian takes his pumpkin carving very seriously) " . . . my sister's pumpkins are . . . "

The door was gently closed on his jack-o-lantern tirade. I'm sure he ended up with at least five houses' worth of candy from the poor woman.

The rest of the year, Ian will talk about which houses gave him candy as we drive or walk by. He keeps an incredibly accurate accounting of who does, or does not, hand out candy, going all the way back to his first Halloween.

I grew up in the city, and my Halloweens were busy affairs. The smell of shaving cream seemed to hover over the crowded streets . . . orange, black and red everywhere. I loved the lights and the noise, the excitement, the rustle of the candy from the bag heavy on my arm, and later the candy spread across the living room floor—a carpet of sugar.

Now Halloween is different. The four of us walk together in the darkness as we look for the next house. Many times we'll get our first gentle rain of the season, and the air will fill with the wonderful scent as the dust of summer is washed away. For my children, the candy bags are only partly full, and there is a different kind of excitement in the air . . . more like anticipation. It is quiet and peaceful. And maybe that's as it should be, a quiet time to mark the end of harvest and the coming of winter—my favorite season.

We walk on together in the soft darkness as the stars peak out between the clouds. I smile to myself . . . the three most important people in my life are beside me, winter is coming, and the next house beckons.

{ 45 }

A Closed Door

I stand outside your door and listen to your tears. You need me by your side to tell you everything is okay, that no matter what, I still love you. Then you will give a gentle sigh of relief and with that sigh you will breathe out the last of the anger, the hate, and the rage, and then you will sleep.

I have stood outside this door many times over your ten years of life, listening and waiting for the right moment to come to you. You've hit me and you've spit at me. You've told me that you hate me and that you want me to leave you. Each time, I've reached out, opened the door, and entered the dark warmth of your room to find you sitting on the edge of your bed. I taste the salt of your tears as I kiss you. I hold you in my arms and stroke your hair, saying the words you so desperately need to hear. I tell you that no matter what you do, I will always love you. I tell you that you are safe. I tell you that I will always be at your side. I tell you that you are good.

Tonight as I stand here listening to your tears, my arm feels heavy . . . too heavy to lift my hand to the doorknob. My tongue feels dead; it is no longer nimble enough to form the words you need to hear. My eyes hurt, for tonight they burn with my own tears. Tonight the dark of your room is the darkness of the pits. Tonight you told me that you wanted to kill me. Sometimes loving you is hard.

I reach out and turn the knob anyway.

{ 46 }

Everything

You take everything I have to give,
and then you ask for more.
I pull it from my bones.

Christmas Films

We have two films that we used to check out from the local library every Christmas for years. The library finally gave them to us because no one else ever used them.

We invite my family over to our house, I make "Christmas Chili" and then we settle in for *Christmas on Grandfather's Farm* and Dylan Thomas's *A Child's Christmas in Wales*. There could not be two more completely opposite films: *Christmas on Grandfather's Farm* is old, corny and wonderful; *A Child's Christmas in Wales* is slow, stately, beautiful.

There is a scene in *Grandfather's Farm* where a young boy receives a colt for Christmas. The scene has become a family tradition; we all say the lines with the boy in the same monotone, laughing at the blank look on his face. "A colt . . . a colt."

This year, the colt scene struck me cold. I suddenly saw Ian in that boy. I said nothing for the rest of the film. As the starkly beautiful sounds of a single flute led us into Dylan Thomas, Ian joined me as I lay on the floor. I was surprised. He'd never shown much interest in the movies. He snuggled up to me; I put my arms around him.

Dylan Thomas's voice, its Welsh accent sounding of cigarettes and bitter beer, washed over me: "One Christmas was much like another in our cold seaside town . . . "

I thought of the boy looking at his colt, of my family's laughter, and, of Ian. I rubbed my face into Ian's hair and wiped the tears from my eyes.

{ 48 }

A Game of Catch

When I added teaching music classes in the afternoons after my kindergarteners went home, I was afraid that it would take the magic away from my own music. I didn't want music to feel like a job. To my surprise I found that I enjoyed it.

One day the fire alarm went off right in the middle of one of my third-grade music classes. It was just a drill, and the kids knew it. The classroom teachers usually left their classes with me and took a break. I could just see the kids going wild in the line; if I had been in their place, I know I would have too. To say that I was "no angel" when I was in school would be putting it mildly.

"I need you guys to be absolutely silent when we go out," I said in my "Serious Teacher" voice. "Go line up at the door."

We walked out into a beautiful spring-like day in the middle of February. A warm wind was blowing, and the air was filled with the scent of grass.

I must have scared them, because they were quiet as we stood there waiting for the bell to ring to signal the okay to return to class.

"Why don't I just take them," their teacher Charlene said, joining us in line as the bell rang. "By the time you've got them settled down again it'll be time to go anyway."

"Ten minutes free play!" She called and her class took off screaming in delight.

I laughed. "I thought you were going to take them back to your room."

"How can I make them sit inside on a day like this?" she said.

"I think I'll stay out too," I said.

It had been a rainy, cold winter; I had loved every minute of it. So if I could appreciate a day like this, I could only imagine what a normal, sun-starved person must be feeling.

It was Thursday, and a three-day weekend beckoned. Char and I stood together in the warm sunshine talking about our plans as her kids played. Ten minutes never went by so fast.

My next class was a small percussion group, three boisterous fifth-grade boys. They were just arriving as I walked back to my classroom. I followed them inside. After the beautiful weather outside, my room felt hot and stuffy. One of the boys had a football under his arm.

"Let's go outside and toss the football around," I said.

"Really?" they asked.

"Sure, it's beautiful out there. Let's go."

As we spread out over the field, I smiled. These stolen moments in the school day are always my favorite. As we threw the ball around, we talked and joked together, the line between teacher and students gradually dissolving until we were just a bunch of guys throwing a football. I'm not a big sports fan, but I was having fun.

I can't wait for Ian to be this age, I thought. *This is wonderful.* Then with a shock I realized, *Ian is this age!*

Even on this beautiful cloudless day heavy with the spring to come—as I watched the ball fly into the vast blue of the sky, soaring and free; as I listened to the laughter of these boys of an age with my son—I felt a weight in my heart.

On this day, I wanted Ian to be normal.

The Redwood Summer Games

Last year we took Ian to the Redwood Summer Games, an annual event for people with special needs. We had no idea what to expect, so instead of staying for the whole Friday through Sunday event, we planned on arriving at ten on Saturday morning and staying through breakfast on Sunday.

On that early Saturday morning in late August, the four of us with our camping gear, drove north on Highway 101. Michelle and Kaylee were excited about camping for the night, and I was looking forward to escaping into the fog from the 100-degree temperatures of August in Lake County. Ian was just worried.

"Will I get to still play my game?" He asked, referring to his video game.

"No, Bug, your game is at home. You can play it tomorrow night when we get back," I said.

"Will I know anyone?"

"I doubt it. We've never been there."

"Will it be fun?"

"We hope so. You said you wanted to go when we asked you about it."

"I don't know if it will be fun," Ian said quietly.

"Let's just give it a chance," I said. "Hey, look at the fog!"

At first glance, I was reminded of the Special Olympics, but in reality the Redwood Games seemed much more casual. The games were held in a beautiful campground in the middle of the coastal redwoods of California. One of the first things that impressed me about the camp was the sense of community; most of the people there seemed to know one another, and most seemed to have been coming to the event for years. The second thing I noticed was the emphasis on fun, not competition. The motto of the games, "All for fun, and fun for all," was definitely apparent.

It was an interesting experience. Many of the participants took the events very seriously, but there was never a feeling of all-out competition. The people in charge did a fantastic job of making everyone feel like winners. Ian was higher-functioning than most of the other participants, and also quite a bit younger, but as we wandered through the day's events—races, free throw contests, ball tosses—Ian seemed to be enjoying himself.

After dinner came the closing night ceremonies. All the contestants received a medal attached to a colorful ribbon, and those who wished to got a chance to talk to the crowd through the announcer's microphone.

When it was Ian's turn, he walked up to the podium, accepted his ribbon like an Olympian receiving the gold, took the microphone, and turned to the crowd. His eyes grew wide when he realized there were over a hundred people staring at him, and I thought he was going to hand the microphone back without saying anything.

"Thank you," he said humbly.

I smiled. We work hard to teach our kids good manners.

"It was kind of boring. I didn't want to come."

I'm sure my eyebrows shot up to the top of my head. I turned to Michelle. She looked horrified. A few people laughed.

"I didn't want to come," (how kind of him to restate that point just in case someone in the crowd hadn't heard the first time), "but my mom and dad made me."

Maybe no one will know he's mine, I thought in desperation.

"I didn't want to come, but I came to try it. I always do what my mom and dad tell me."

Laughing, the announcer took the microphone from Ian's hand and joked about how he wished his own kids would do what he told them to.

Ian proudly strutted back to us, winding his way through the crowd, and just to be sure everyone noticed, waving the ribbon over his head like a flag. We hastily headed back to our tent.

On the way to the bathroom to brush my teeth the following morning, I wandered around the campground a bit. I noticed that the vast majority of campsites were large groups from group homes, many with colorful banners proudly displayed.

I went on to the bathroom, turned on the tap, and began to brush; the frigid water gurgling down the drain.

I just want to get out of here, I thought, *with no one recognizing Ian.*

As I was finishing up, in walked a man who was perhaps in his twenties. Although he was non-verbal, he proudly showed off the medal he'd won the night before. He was so excited. He clearly needed to show off his prize. I remembered how proud he'd been last night—indeed how proud and excited they all had been—practically dancing on the stage as he scanned the crowd. We left the bathroom together and walked down the path back to the campgrounds, where he turned towards one of the group camps.

I called to him, "Congratulations on your medal!"

Dancing from foot to foot, he smiled and waved the medal above his head, then he entered one of the four tents that made up his campsite. A flag with "Sequoia House" written on it fluttered in the breeze above the tents.

I suddenly felt sad. I wondered how many of those people last night had been lucky enough to look out into that crowd and see the proud faces of their parents there to support them. I looked around me at the sea of group home camps.

Not many, I thought.

My embarrassment from the night before vanished. I turned and went to find Ian.

I don't know where Ian will end up in this life, but I do know that he will always have us . . . proud parents watching him from the crowd.

{ 50 }

Aunt Margie

Michelle's aunt died the other day. She was a wonderful woman, but the first time I met her, I wasn't so sure.

It was our wedding day, and my friend Tom and I were hanging up signs at the top of the long driveway leading down to my parents' house where we were holding the wedding. Up came a van, and upon seeing us, the driver slowed to a stop and rolled down the window. The man in the driver's seat didn't even get a chance to speak before a woman lunged across him as he tried his best to get out of her way. I had an image of eyes that I swear were shooting bolts of lightning, and framed by curly hair the color of steel.

"Where in the world is this house we're supposed to find? We've been driving since Sacramento, and this map is useless! You need signs out here so people know where they're going! And what about my salad?"

I pointed to the sign I'd just hung, but she didn't seem to notice. I thought it safer not to ask about the salad.

"We've been driving around for hours. I've got a macaroni salad in the back there; it's probably gone bad!"

I smiled meekly, nodded in sympathy about the macaroni salad, and pointed again at the sign.

"Mayonnaise can't sit out this long, especially in this heat!"

I was beginning to feel a bit warm myself. I ran a finger around the collar of my tux.

"Well?"

I just stared blankly.

"WELL?"

I turned to Tom for help. He looked a little pale.

"WHERE IS THE HOUSE!" she bellowed.

Then she noticed the sign, said something to the driver, and sat back in her seat mumbling about the salad. The driver, who I later learned was Uncle Bob, smiled apologetically and drove off. He hadn't said a word . . . neither had I. Tom and I just stood there watching them drive off with our ears ringing.

"Are you sure you want to marry into this family?" Tom said.

"I think so, but I know one thing. I'm not touching that macaroni salad."

As it turned out, the salad was wonderful. The rest of the food had run out by the time Michelle and I were ready to eat—it was macaroni salad or starve.

Aunt Margie and I bonded over that macaroni salad, and our relationship evolved into what she dubbed "Hank's Salad"—broccoli, cauliflower, a sweet dressing—marvelous stuff.

She must have been having a bad day when I met her, because I never saw that side of her again. As a matter of fact, she was one of the few people whom we could feel completely at ease with after we had Ian. She accepted and loved him as he was, unconditionally. Ian responded to her in kind.

When we told him that she had died, Ian's first reaction was to try and make Michelle feel better.

"Is she in heaven, Dad?"

"I'm sure she is."

"She's beautiful now, Mom. She can see us."

Michelle was crying, and Ian went up to her and put his arm around her.

"You don't need to cry, Mom, it'll be okay."

"Mommy needs to be sad right now," I said. "We just need to give her some time, and she'll be okay."

"Is it like how Uncle Pete can see us, but we can't see him?"

"Yeah, Ian, it's like that," I said, "but just like Uncle Pete, she'll always be around."

Ian turned again to Michelle. "I'm going to buy a telescope, and we can look up at Aunt Margie and see her, and she'll wave to us."

It was time for bed, and as I was turning off the light, Ian sighed heavily.

"Are you thinking about Aunt Margie?" I asked.

"Yeah, but I'm not going to cry."

"It's okay to cry. I do, a lot."

He sighed again.

"Think about that telescope," I said and closed the door.

One of my favorite poems is called "Questions About Angels" by Billy Collins. He has wonderful images in there: a lone angel dancing the night away to a jazz combo; an angel falling off a cloud into a river and making a hole that slowly drifts downstream; angels rowing in boats while looking down at us as we go through our days. I'd like to add Ian's image to those of Billy Collins—dear Aunt Margie, waving to us from heaven with a bowl of macaroni salad in her hand.

My son has the soul of a poet.

Autism Is...

Autism is coming home and finding Michelle crying on the couch.
. . . it's a disapproving look, and a judgment from a stranger.
. . . it's rage, a rage that strikes out, bites deep, and finds bone.

Autism is Ian sitting at home alone and beginning to understand why.
. . . it's not being invited to birthday parties.
. . . it's being the butt of the joke.

Autism is trying to make sense of a world that moves too fast.
. . . it's too many words, and too much sound.
. . . it's wanting, and not knowing how to receive.

Autism is fear.
. . . it's fear of the future.
. . . it's fear of tomorrow.

Autism is . . .
a gentle soul, and sweet innocence,
profound moments, and beautiful words,
gentleness, and unlooked-for strength . . .

Autism is Ian . . . always . . . forever.

{ 52 }

Family Photos

"I wish Aunt Margie could come back like he does," Ian said pointing at the TV.

One of the characters had died at the beginning of the film and was coming back to life here at the end.

"I do too, Bug," I said. "I wish Uncle Pete could come back too."

My brother died when his fishing boat sank off the coast of California. I was a sophomore in high school at the time. The school year was almost over, and he was on his way to pick me up for a summer on the boat.

We have a picture of Pete hanging on the wall above our dining room table. He stands at the bow of the boat. His long, nicotine-stained fingers grasp the railing, narrow face, crooked grin; a long blonde ponytail tucked over his shoulder. Ian and Kaylee often look at it and ask me questions about him. How I wish that they could have known him.

I look at the picture too, and remember . . .

Pete pulls into the driveway of our house for a visit. All of ten years old at the time, I dash out to his car, and he hugs me tight. I remember the feel of his long, skinny body, the rough worn jacket against my face, the smell of cigarettes and coffee.

It is springtime, and we are driving through Muir Woods on the way to the coast to meet Pete. A spicy eucalyptus smell flows through the car. When we arrive, we find *Lincoln* docked beside a restaurant there on the wharf. I remember how proud I feel as I climb onto the boat beneath the eyes of tourists in the window seats with their watchful eyes and crab-stuffed cheeks.

And I remember the last time I heard Pete's voice, on a crackling phone line from some fishing port who knows where. I picture the fog rolling in and I can almost see Pete's lanky form in the phone booth; the glowing ash falls from the cigarette as he hops from foot to foot for warmth.

"I love you," he says.

"What?"

"I said, I love you."

I am embarrassed. I make some silly comment in return to cover it and hand the phone to Mom for her turn.

That night I sit at my desk and write him a letter. I tell him how proud I am to have him for a brother, how much I look up to him, and that I love him. The words stare accusingly at me from the page. They are words that should have been spoken aloud, not trusted to the mail.

I am haunted by the thought that he may never have had the chance to read them.

***

At the end of Ian's fourth-grade school year, his class went on a field trip to the coast for whale watching. I took the day off to join them. As the school bus wound its way down to the docks, I pointed to a long, narrow strip of land that divides the entrance to the harbor in two— almost like lanes on a divided road.

"Ian, does that look familiar?"

"What, where?" he asked, pressing his face to the window.

"There, the channel leading out to the ocean," I said, pointing and trying to think of a better word for channel.

"You mean with the ground in the middle?"

"Yeah . . . have you ever seen that before?"

Ian looked at it doubtfully.

"We've got a picture of it above our dining room table," I said.

"You mean Uncle Pete?"

"Yep, that's where that picture was taken."

Ian was quiet until we were getting off the bus.

"Uncle Pete was here?" he asked.

"Yeah, this was one of the places he'd stop to unload fish."

"I miss Uncle Pete."

"Yeah, Ian, I do too. I wish you could have known him."

We climbed onto the boat and headed out to sea. I felt strange traveling along a route that would have been old and familiar to Pete. When we were well out to sea, I looked back at the coastline, trying to pick out the spot where he died. His last hours of life were spent on these seas.

You can see where he died from shore; the rocks stand out of the waves like teeth. I always think of *Lincoln*, still out there somewhere. I went there for the first time with Michelle, and while we strolled along the shore, I picked up two stones from the beach. I kept them for years on a shelf in my music studio until Ian and Kaylee were born. These rocks now sit in their bedrooms, and I touch them each night as I kiss my sleeping children good night. I like the thought of them there, sitting through the long hours of the night; Pete watching over my children and keeping them safe.

Pete was a writer, a poet mostly, and I wonder what he would think if he could read these words I've labored over for so long. I can't help but fear he would find them silly and juvenile. For although I am now much older than he ever had the chance to be, he will forever be the adult, and I the child. That child in me still craves his approval and hopes that he'd find something here of worth.

There is another photograph, and in it I stand looking at a statue of a fisherman; two-year-old Ian is in my arms. I am crying as I find Pete's name among the names of so many fishermen whose lives are gone. We look so much alike, my son and I. We wear identical sweaters, and it is as if our bodies are one. Ian is pointing to the plaque with one chubby finger.

I find it sad to think about because it is so bleak . . . so final. An entire life, recorded on film from its very beginning to its end. The photographs that are gathered together and placed in an album with loving care. Perhaps a hand reaches out, a tentative finger touching the image of a face long gone but well remembered. A teardrop is carefully brushed away lest it damage the film, and then the album is closed and placed upon a shelf. An entire life bound within the covers of a book.

But, as has happened many times before, I find solace in thoughts of Ian.

I remember his first experience with death when his hamster died. As we put his hamster into the hole we'd dug in the yard, the body stiff and cold, I hesitated, as I always do. I was afraid of the awful finality of that first shovelful of dirt.

Ian turned to me with moist eyes.

"This is the last time I'll see him," he said.

"Yes, Ian, it is."

"I want him to come back," he said, and then the tears came.

I remember wishing I could have shielded him from that pain, but soon after, Aunt Margie died and, as is his way with things, he tied it all together.

"Aunt Margie won't come back, huh?"

"You're right, she won't."

"She's with Uncle Pete and Grandpa Ross in heaven . . . and my hamsters."

"Yeah, that's right, she is," I said.

I love the way Ian thinks sometimes. What an image . . . Michelle's father, Aunt Margie, and Pete sitting around on some heavenly cloud, playing with hamsters.

53

Stones on a Windowsill

I watch us, Pete and I, flickering in the uncertain light of the old family movie. I'm on my tricycle; Pete is standing on the back. We are driving me through a maze of old metal buckets. Although the film is silent but for the chatter of the old projector, I hear the laughter as I remember that day.

I remember playing "King Gets"as Pete tackles me to the floor, and tickles me as I fall. The game of "King Gets" lives on now with Ian and Kaylee, and I always think of Pete as I throw them to the ground in happy abandon.

I miss you Pete. I wish that you were here to share my children with me. I wish I could talk to you about my demons, for I feel that you of all people would truly understand. And I wish you could know my autistic son.

I miss my brother . . . stones on a windowsill are a poor substitute.

54

The Haircut

With Ian, sometimes the most mundane things become wonderful. Ian and Kaylee had an appointment for a haircut after school. I met Michelle and the kids at the shop so Michelle could run a few errands.

"Hi, Judy!" Ian walked up and gave her a hug. Judy is a small woman, and Ian is a big kid; he dwarfed her.

Kaylee settled herself into a chair, nose buried in a book.

She's taken care of, I thought and smiled.

I found a chair for myself. There was an interview in one of the

magazines with a composer I like. I'd never seen an interview with him before, and I was excited about reading it.

"Have you ever seen the Spiderman movie?" Ian asked.

"No, I haven't," Judy answered as she led him to a chair.

"Why not?" Ian sounded amazed.

"Well, I guess I'm not really interested in Spiderman. Have you seen it?"

"My mom and dad are deciding if it's appropriate for me. I have the Spiderman game for my Game Cube. I beat the last boss. He was the Green Goblin. You have to get extra lives to get him. Then I . . . "

The sentences were coming so fast they were running into each other. I looked up from my magazine; Judy was smiling. She's known Ian since birth and is great with him.

"Dad, you're deciding if it's appropriate right . . . huh, right?" Ian loves the word *appropriate*; he'll whisper it to himself, rolling it around on his tongue.

"We're still talking about it," I said and went back to my reading to a background drone about Spiderman.

"Is a thousand more than a hundred?" I looked up, realizing there'd been a shift in topic. He was still talking to Judy, so I went back to my magazine.

"Yes, a thousand is lots more."

"How much more is a million?"

"A lot more than a thousand."

"I'm the Math King at school; my teacher Mrs. Chase told me."

"What grade are you in now?"

"I'm fifthshould'vebeensixth." (Translation: fifth, should've been sixth. To Ian it's all one word.) "Mom and Dad kept me back in fourth grade, but I . . ."

The conversation went on. I tried to concentrate on my magazine, but it was getting harder.

"Ian, what happened to your hair?" Judy asked. Ian stopped talking. "Did someone cut it?"

I put down my magazine. Judy was laughing. Ian looked sheepish.

"It was in my way. I cut it."

Judy showed me where a good two inches had been cut off near the top of his head.

Maybe I can borrow the magazine, I thought to myself. *This is too good to miss.*

"My grandma gets her hair cut in here. She lives by the lake. I swim there and . . . " Ian was off again.

"I'm going to be a grandma, Ian."

He looked at her.

"Are you old?" he asked, plainly shocked.

Judy laughed. "Well, I guess I'm old enough to be a grandma."

Ian reached out and stroked her face. "But you're smooth."

Judy turned to me, laughing. "I love your son."

"Grandma and Grandpa take us to the Christmas Hotel and . . . "

Michelle arrived to take over with Kaylee. Ian headed outside.

"How'd he do?" Michelle asked.

"It was wonderful," I said.

I went out to find Ian. The shop is on a fairly busy road. It was five o'clock, and lots of people were heading home from work. There was Ian, standing under a tree. He'd found a large branch and was strutting along the side of the road holding it over his head, pretending to be a deer . . . gloriously oblivious to the startled looks of the drivers.

"Come on Ian, let's head for the truck."

"Can I take my stick, Dad? Why are you smiling?"

It was while we were driving that I realized I'd forgotten the magazine. I guess some things just aren't that important.

{ 55 }

Brain Scan

I remember standing at Ian's side, sealed together in a small, sterile metal room. Ian was splayed out on the table, electrodes attached to his head, repeating meaningless sounds that came with robotic precision over the speaker from the world outside.

"Boo pah. Pah bah."

They wanted to find out why his brain works the way it does. He was required to lie absolutely still. Promised prizes awaited outside that steel tomb, they dangled there like carrots on a stick to buy his acquiescence. He was an object to them, a scientific oddity, potential data to be added to a report.

We used to think it important to have a label for Ian; a word to use to describe what he is. But on that day as I stood there in the tomblike silence that lay between the meaningless words and watched as he struggled to lie still so that they would let him out into the air and the sun again, on that day, I ceased to care anymore.

56

White Coats and Sterilized Rooms

Doctor after doctor, we made the rounds like so many desperate parents before us. We were searching for a cure, a label, a reason . . . desperate for reassurance. We wanted a doctor who would tell us why, and how, and when. A doctor who would open his book, and say, "Here's what you need to do," with complete confidence and authority, like a priest in his pulpit, with his bible and his God.

Instead we found a psychiatrist who talked to Ian for ten minutes and pronounced him ADHD, a team of doctors who said they'd never seen anyone like him, and a developmental pediatrician who wanted us to drug the magic out of him.

There were others, some good and some bad, but the more people we saw, the more we came to realize that there really were no answers out there. And so we set the search aside, set aside the doctors with their white coats and sterilized rooms.

Then, and only then, did we find the magic and the beauty that was there all along. Trust in ourselves, and in our son, finally brought us the tools to pull the diamond from the slag.

Now our work begins.

57

Puberty

"Hank, come here a minute," Michelle called.

"Hang on a sec, I've got raw chicken all over."

So far it had been a nice quiet evening, I was in the middle of cooking dinner, Kaylee was busily playing in her room, and Ian was in the shower.

"Come now." Michelle's voice sounded odd. "You need to see this."

She was standing outside the bathroom door, which was open a crack. Ian had just finished his shower and was standing there in the warm mist, drying himself.

"What's wrong?"

"Well, nothing . . . look at Ian."

"What . . . what's wrong?"

"*Nothing* . . . look!"

At first I couldn't figure out what she was talking about. Ian continued drying himself off, completely oblivious . . . and then I saw. Ian had pubic hair; my eleven-year-old was starting puberty!

It's funny how as a parent you are so intimately aware of your child's body as you bathe them and change them. The scent of baby wipes or baby powder—the crinkling of a disposable diaper —can instantly transport me to days long gone. But as children grow and become more and more independent, this awareness fades, until suddenly, as on this day, one is shocked.

And I *was* shocked. This outward sign of Ian's budding maturity seemed an impostor, an intruder in my son's innocent body. I was surprised at my reaction. I consider myself very open sexually, but I found myself awash in emotion.

Ian looked up and noticed me standing there. I pretended to examine the doorjamb. He finished drying, hung up his towel, and headed to his room.

"Hey, Dad," he said as he walked by.

"Hey, Bug," I said. *What's wrong with me?* I thought. *It's just pubic hair . . . no big deal.*

But it felt like a big deal, and I didn't know why.

The next day at school, I was talking to my friend Arden. I told her about Ian, and how strange I felt.

"It's because he's getting older," Arden said. She mentioned something about her teenage son and driving. He had been in my kindergarten class years ago.

"God, that makes me feel old!" I said.

"What does?"

"David driving. He was just in kindergarten."

"How do you think it makes me feel?" she said. "I'm his mom."

I walked out of her room feeling depressed, and again I didn't know why.

There's something about driving. Maybe it's the quiet mindlessness of it, but I find my brain works best as I drive to or from work, a 35-minute commute with absolutely no traffic. That day, while driving home, I thought of Ian beginning to mature, and I thought of David driving.

God, that'll be next, Ian driving! I thought, and then I had it . . . I finally realized what was bothering me.

It wasn't just about Ian getting older. It was about Ian "the autistic" getting older.

Growing up is hard for any kid, but it is probably harder on their parents. Much of the talk I hear in my teachers' room at school revolves around our kids, and everyone is quick with their advice— some good, some bad—but the point of it all is not really the advice, it's the comfort of hearing someone else say, "Yeah, we went through that with our son."

I don't have that luxury.

"Ian turned sixteen yesterday. Can autistics get a driver's license?"

"Ian asked me why he's different from other kids. When did you first tell your son that he was autistic?"

"They're having a dance at Ian's school. He asked a girl to go but she laughed at him. How do I tell him that some 'normal' girls probably won't be interested?"

"His friends have outgrown him. They don't want to play tag or talk about Disney films or play video games. Nobody wants to have him spend the night, and no one wants to come over to our house. I don't know what to do."

I know that Ian feels alone and left out at times. Sometimes I do too.

{ 58 }

Selfish Dreams

Since childhood, I've had a dream of living in England. The rain, the cloaking mists, the endless green moors—they appeal to that part of me that cries for anonymity and to the winter in my soul. I applied to teach there when I first got my credential, but they would not accept first-year teachers. Then marriage and children changed the course of my life, and that dream was set aside. I once talked to Michelle about teaching in England for a year as part of an exchange program. She was hesitant at first.

"It would be a great experience for the kids," I said, and she seemed to agree, albeit reluctantly.

Then Ian was diagnosed with autism. Consistency became of supreme importance in our life; any change in routine was extremely difficult. Thinking of moving to another country for a year was impossible; that dream too was set aside.

And so my dreams have turned to the sea. I've always loved the coast. Perhaps the rain and fog remind me of England. Perhaps it is because my brother spent most of his life there and died there as well. I've always felt closest to him when I'm standing on the shore with the waves washing across my booted feet, the cold, salt air catching at my throat.

Hank Smith

***

Last night was a bad night. I put Ian to bed, wanting only to be left alone. I went to sleep and dreamed of England.

I am walking through an infinite green field, feeling good for the movement. I walk into the mists that roll across the hills, and they cover me like a well-worn sweater, smelling of earth . . . and the sea.

This morning was bad too. Ian was loud and belligerent, sharp-edged and brittle. I put him into Michelle's car, placed a quick kiss on the top of his head, and got into my truck. The half-hour drive felt good. It was quiet, and I was alone—almost like walking through the fields of my dream. I came to the intersection: a right turn takes me to my school, to the life I've chosen for myself; a left turn leads to the coast. My hands tightened on the steering wheel, daring me to turn left.

My mind races ahead . . . to an imaginary cottage alone on a cliff. Sighing grasses surround it for miles, and the sea crashes at the cliff's foot. I can almost taste the salt and feel the mists as they prick goose bumps on my skin. In my mind I pull well-worn boots onto my feet and walk out into the grass. I walk, and walk, and walk . . . there is no one there to stop me. No one there to tell me what to do, no yelling, no noise . . . no responsibilities. I walk for miles . . . for days, for years. I lose myself in the sweet, soft gray of the fog.

A truck blew the mists away with a choking cloud of diesel and pulled me back to reality. Gone was the cottage on the cliff, the crashing sea, and the miles of grass bent before the wind.

I gripped the wheel and turned right.

Set Aside

Kaylee handed me her grading sheet for the city report she had worked on for the past three weeks. 100 percent. Her face glowed with pride as I pulled her to me and kissed her lavender-scented hair.

Later, I found her reading in my chair, absorbed in a book. In the golden glow of the lamp, I saw the baby who suddenly had become a young girl and who all too soon would be a woman.

In the maelstrom of our autistic life, I sometimes wonder . . . does she feel as though she is set aside?

{ 60 }

Anxiety

The thoughts whirl about inside my mind like a tornado and are just as destructive: insecurities about my music and my writing, that mole on Michelle's shoulder. Just as I grasp one worry and try to deal with it, it swirls away in the maelstrom, a leaf in the gale, and is quickly replaced by another. The anxieties attack everything that is important to me, everything I care about. Michelle, the kids—nothing is safe from my demons. They hate me as much as I hate them.

I go to Michelle. I want to know if she is still attracted to this forty-two-year-old man she married so long ago. I've asked the question many times before, and the rational side of my mind knows the answer, but I need to hear an outside voice giving familiar words of comfort. This night she explodes in frustration, and I withdraw into my shell. It is lonely here and dark.

Kaylee calls out, unable to sleep, worried about something that happened at school. She's asked the questions many times already, but needs to ask them again; she too needs to hear an outside voice. I say the words, and she is comforted, rolls over and sleeps.

I go to Ian, stand and watch his sleeping face—released for now from his obsessions. I stand there for a long time and then I go to bed.

Michelle is there for me now, and her arms surround me. Her

words of comfort soothe, but as I drift into sleep I am afraid.

    My children are so like me, and they follow in my footsteps down this dark road. I need to guide them back to the daylight.

{ 61 }

Walking the Dogs

I'd been working for the past four months remodeling our bathroom. It had been quite a job, literally down to the floorboards, and as a result I hadn't been spending much time with the kids. It was a Sunday, and Michelle was at a dance convention for the weekend. I was deep in the bowels of the house hammering away when Ian and Kaylee came to me.

"Dad, we're bored!" said Kaylee.

"Yeah," said Ian.

My standard response of late had been to tell them to turn on a movie, but this time guilt got the better of me.

"How about a walk?" I asked.

Soon we were underway with our two dogs in tow. It was a beautiful day, and I realized how good it felt to be out of the house. The air was crisp and clear and held a hint of the bite of winter, my favorite time of year. Soon these walks would turn into what we call puddle walks; walks in the pouring rain in search of the deepest puddles we can find until we're soaked to the skin. Then it's home again to mugs of hot chocolate and tea. I long for those grey, stormy days and, best of all, the long cold nights safe inside with a book while the wind and the rain rage outside.

"Dad, what's all over your pants?" Kaylee broke into my reverie.

I looked down. At best, one might say that my work clothes look pretty awful—stains and rips everywhere—but during the course of working on the bathroom, I'd discovered a wonderful thing.

Whenever I'm working and need to write something down, I never seem to have any paper nearby. I've always got a pen because I keep one in my tool belt, but never any paper. Usually I use a scrap of lumber to write on, but one day I discovered that I could just write stuff down on my clothes. They looked so hideous anyway that it really didn't matter. As a result, on this day, I was wearing four months' worth of shopping lists for the lumber yard, odd measurements, and diagrams—some bits scribbled out, some almost faded away from repeated washings, others standing out proudly, bright and new.

I looked at Kaylee, and she didn't look much better. She had on clothes that were so mismatched that even I could tell. In fact, if she moved around too quickly, I felt vaguely nauseated.

"Kaylee, I wouldn't talk. You don't look so great yourself." Then I looked at Ian. He was peacefully clomping along holding one of the dogs' leashes.

He was clomping because he was wearing a pair of my black Wellington boots that were at least 100 sizes too big for him. He'd picked out a pair of grey sweat pants, which would have been fine except that he was wearing them inside-out (he's got this thing about scratchy clothes against his skin). To top off the ensemble, he'd chosen one of Michelle's "I Love Teddy Bears" T-shirts. I realized that no one's hair had been combed that morning, and I'm sure I had a fair amount of sawdust and bits of sheetrock in mine. We were quite a sight.

Well, chances are we won't run into anyone, I thought. Our walks tend to be solitary affairs. Today that was not to be.

We rounded a corner. A car passed, then another, and another. I was sure each had slowed down a bit to take in the view, or perhaps they expected one of us to suddenly wail like a Banshee and jump in front of their car. We had started up the last hill before the downward slope to home when a woman appeared walking towards us. She had a dog as well. Passing another dog on our walks has always been a great moment in Cooter's and Sebastian's lives. They began tugging on their leashes and making horrible choking sounds as they tried vainly to reach the woman's dog.

Ian immediately launched into his dog speech.

"Don't worry, our dogs are on leashes, they're friendly, their names are Cooter and Sebastian, they don't bite, my name's Ian, I'm nine, my sister's name is Kaylee, this is my dad, we play rough on weekends, but I always win."

It went on and on and on, the ultimate run-on sentence, with a vast amount of information and, for all the woman knew, a test to follow.

Her smile was rather fixed as she edged quickly to the other side of the road. I could only imagine what she was thinking. Here she was, taking a peaceful walk on a beautiful day when she runs into a group of lunatics dressed in their best finery; leading two gasping, ravenous hounds; and she is assaulted with more information than any sane person would ever care to hear.

Kaylee was skittering across the pavement, vainly holding on to the leash. I quickly stepped forward to help. The woman moved onto the graveled edge of the road. A huge poison oak bush loomed over her head; she didn't seem to care. I grabbed the leash from Kaylee's hand and, with a mighty tug, brought the dogs to heel. Ian gave her a cheery wave of his hand and we moved on.

As we reached the top of the hill, I turned. The woman was still watching us from the bottom. I wondered what was going through her mind. I've also wondered if she ever walked that way again.

Doorknobs and Latches

Sometimes Ian embarrasses the hell out of me.

I have a good friend whom I have known since the seventh grade. I've known him so long that he seems like part of the family. In fact, to Ian and Kaylee he is known as Uncle Tom.

Tom is an interesting guy. An artist at heart, he had made quite a bit of money during the computer boom of the '80s and bought a home in the heart of Silicon Valley in the San Francisco Bay Area. He quit work around ten years ago, found some people to rent his house, grew a ponytail, and retreated to Northern California. He has lived there ever since on the rental income. He spends his days painting and studying and writing about a philosopher he is interested in. His nights are a different story.

Tom has been crafting a spectacular beer belly for the past ten years or so. He puts only the finest beer into it and does so with great gusto. After a long day of philosophizing, he walks with purposeful intent to the local brewpub, sidles up to the bar, and goes to work. After a few pints, he walks back home, where the whole process begins again.

Ian loves Tom, and Tom is one of those rare people we feel completely comfortable with, no matter how Ian is behaving. Tom accepts and loves Ian as he is, even after, I hope, the "baby question."

"Hi, Uncle Tom!" Ian yelled with delight, as Tom arrived for a weekend visit.

"Hi Ian, how've you been doing?"

Ian didn't answer; he just pointed to our deck door.

"Doorknob," he said.

Tom knows this game well. "Doorknob," he answered seriously.

"Latch," said Ian.

"Latch," said Tom.

For years this has been their private greeting. I have no idea how it started, but in my opinion it's completely bizarre (even for an autistic and a forty-two-year-old artist/philosopher/retired computer wiz).

After they'd finished their in-depth discussion of the intricacies of our deck door, Ian paused, staring at Tom. He looked very serious.

"Uncle Tom?" he asked.

"Yes, Ian?"

Ian paused and reached out a tentative hand to touch Tom's stomach.

"Do you have a baby in there?" he asked solemnly.

I don't remember Tom's response. I was making an embarrassed break for the door. After all, I know all the parts, " . . . doorknob, latch."

***

"I'm not going to be able to make it down for Ian's birthday," Tom said on the phone.

"Don't worry about it," I said. "We've still got a lot of people coming."

When I hung up, I went to find Ian.

"Bug, Uncle Tom can't come to your birthday."

"Oh, man!" Ian said in disappointment.

"He said to tell you that he'll be coming to spend the night soon though, in just a couple of weeks."

"Okay," Ian said.

I thought it had all been forgotten, until a Thursday morning a few weeks later. Sometimes I think Ian has a sixth sense.

"When's Uncle Tom coming?"

"Well, Ian, actually he's coming tonight."

Ian's face brightened. "To stay?"

"Yep."

"For two nights?"

"Nope, just one night this time."

Tom arrived in time for dinner. Ian ran up to him and handed him a note.

My Uncle Tom is coming to spend the night at my house. He might give us some treats. But he didn't come to my birthday party. He might give a birthday present for me. But if he didn't, that's okay.

Dear Uncle Tom,

You are certainly invited to my house to stay. You get to see Kaylee and I this time. After dinner, we can have family game night. I hope you have fun with us.

From,

Ian

Tom laughed. The birthday present was under his arm; the treats were gummi bears and jellybeans. Dinner was pizza, followed by a rousing game of *Sorry*. Ian went to bed happy and content . . . so did I.

Ian and I have some pretty wonderful people in our lives, I thought as I drifted off.

{ 63 }

The Football Game

We were at a high school football game watching Kaylee cheer. She'd been to a weeklong cheerleader camp for young girls, and this was her big night. Ian was with us and not at all pleased to have been dragged away from his Friday night routine. Ian's Fridays usually begin with extra video game time followed by dinner on trays in front of a movie.

Once we got to our seats in the bleachers, Ian perked up a bit and began asking questions about the game. I have absolutely no interest in sports. It's funny how people assume that if you're a man, you like sports. Over the years, I've become quite good at carrying on long conversations about sports without having the faintest idea what I'm talking about. A well placed "Mmm, yeah!" or a "Whoa, man!" go a long way.

I tried to answer Ian's questions as best I could, but it didn't help that we were surrounded by raving football fanatics who, I imagined, were listening in on my answers, pitying the boy who had to live with an ignorant idiot like me. What a picture we must have made—a man with no idea how to play the game explaining football to his autistic son.

I love my daughter dearly, but as far as I'm concerned, after one cheer, you've pretty much seen them all. Soon Ian and I were eyeing the clock; to our dismay we realized that the damn thing kept stopping when someone got tackled. The twelve-minute quarters soon stretched well past twenty minutes.

"Uhh!" Ian moaned as the clock stopped yet again.

"Hang in there, Bug" I said. "Let's think about dinner."

We had plans to go to McDonalds after the game, one of Ian's favorite places to eat (Hamburger Happy Meal, just ketchup on the burger please, with lemonade). To be honest it's one of my favorite places as well (a Quarter Pounder with cheese, large fries, a Filet of Fish, and a coke); we go so rarely that I gorge myself— it all gets worried off anyway. But you can only talk about the glories of an extremely high-fat meal for just so long, though, and we were soon watching the clock again.

There was an exciting bit where the ambulance driver on duty had to leave on a call and threatened over the loudspeaker to smash past the poor guy who had parked in his way. To our disappointment, an embarrassed man came running up at the last minute to save his car from destruction.

Thankfully, Kaylee only cheered for the first half, and after the longest forty-six minutes and thirty-four seconds of our lives, we were free.

As we all headed to our car, I turned to Ian. "So, Ian, what did you think of your first football game?"

Ian, ever the diplomat, said, "I liked it, but I didn't love it."

"Would you like to go to another sometime?" as the words came out, I suddenly had a horrible thought . . . *You fool! What if he says yes?*

To my immense relief, a hunted look came over Ian's face, his eyes growing large.

"No, Dad!"

A choir of angels couldn't have sounded better. I smiled and put an arm around him as we headed off to wallow in the wonder that is McDonalds. We had earned it.

{ 64 }

Sticks and Stones

Ian trudged up the driveway, carrying his latest stick behind him. Perhaps the word "carrying" should be changed to "dragging," as his latest acquisition was actually a log. He was beginning to realize the full load-capacity of my truck, and with that realization came a whole new world of potential in his eternal stick quest. He leaned his find with the others beside our front door and went inside.

I stood there for a moment gazing at his collection. In Ian's mind, they were much more than just sticks. Swords, boomerangs, antlers, horns from fearsome dinosaurs—they all jostled for position next to the French door. A whole imaginary world leaning there against the house.

The pile was starting to slide towards the door, so I began to gather them into a more orderly stack, and as I did so, I thought of my own collection.

I have stones that I have collected over the years from various times and places in my life. They are tucked here and there throughout our yard, in the house, and even in my truck. Like Ian with his sticks, I find comfort in them. I like the cool weight as I roll them about in my hand, and for a while they take me away from my cares. They even calm me on the dark days when my anxieties scream away in my head.

"Sticks and stones may break your bones" went the childhood

chant in my mind as I stood there in the cold winter afternoon as the light faded away. The wind was coming up; the scent of rain was in the air. "But your words will never hurt me." I turned and entered the house.

Michelle was out, Kaylee was at a friend's for the night, and I'd promised Ian a movie, so soon we were in the truck again heading up to the video store, winding our way out of the hollow in which we live.

The store was crowded, a storm was on the way, and people were ready to settle in with a video or two. Ian headed off to the children's section to look for his movie as I searched for a film for Michelle and I.

Through the noise of the other customers, I could hear Ian muttering to himself as he looked for his video, quoting lines from the movie that he intended to rent in a sort of monotone.

"Kevin, you're all right kid... all right kid... kid... kid."

He rambled on contentedly to himself, and I smiled as I listened.

He's got that movie memorized, and he wants it again, I thought to myself.

It was the giggling that made me turn. Two boys, roughly Ian's age, were standing nearby mocking him. My happiness of a moment ago turned to cold ash. I quickly got Ian, paid for the movies, and hustled him back to the truck. The wind was up, and the last leaves of fall skittered across the parking lot as the first drops of rain pattered against the windshield.

Ian happily chattered away about his movie as we wound back down into the safety of our hollow. Michelle was home, and light spilled from the French doors catching crystal raindrops in midair. We climbed from the truck and ran to the house through the soaking rain. Ian's sticks stood there in the moist light; the rain dripping from them like tears.

For Ian and I, sticks and stones are a balm to our souls in a world that is all too often cold and cruel. The sticks and stones don't break our bones. It's the words that hurt. They bite deep.

{ 65 }

Magic

Along with Ian's autism comes magic: his beautiful innocence; his sense of wonder; his way of looking at ordinary events and making them special. He walks his own path, often turning left as the rest of the world turns right.

Sadly, my son lives in a world of straight lines and neutral colors; a world where magic has no place. The older he gets, the more he stands apart. The older he gets, the more he is shunned.

My instinct as a father is to protect and shelter Ian from this world. My job as a father is to let him learn to deal with it.

Sometimes I hate my job.

Ghosts of Christmas Past

"Hank, you've got to hear this!" Michelle's face was glowing. "It's the latest 'Ian story' from Laurie."

Michelle gets a lot of these 'Ian stories' from his teacher. This was one of the best.

Ian was sitting in class a few weeks before Christmas when a classmate leaned over and said, "Ian, there's no such thing as Santa Claus . . . he's your mom."

Ian paused for a few moments, mulling this concept around in his head.

"No, my mom is a kindergarten teacher . . . you're just confused," he said calmly, and returned to his work.

Ian is almost twelve, and he still believes in Santa Claus. I'm not talking about a boy who wants to believe, or one who's heard his friends' jaded talk but is not ready to give it up. Ian genuinely believes.

Ian's beautiful innocence about Santa Claus has been wonderful because he has drawn Kaylee right along with him. Even though she is nine years old and has started hearing the rumblings of her friends who are beginning to have doubts, Kaylee still seems willing to believe.

We start the holidays with a trip to a local Christmas-tree farm. We take hours and roam through the hills to find just the right tree. It's a beautiful place, no houses in sight, and frequently no people either. The air, cold and clear, puddles from the rain just waiting to be stomped through.

When the tree is finally chosen, Ian and Kaylee help to cut it down. The wonderful spice scent of pine engulfs us at the first cut, and we take turns sawing away until, with a wondrous crack, the tree swishes to the ground.

We are usually heading back to the truck when the annual debate begins.

"Ian, you can't take all those sticks home," is Michelle's traditional opening shot.

We have a huge group of them leaning beside our front door like sheaves of wheat, many from Christmases past, and to Ian, each holds a special meaning.

"Put three back," Michelle will say.

"I don't know which ones."

"How 'bout that one?"

"No! That's a boomerang." He's got a real boomerang, but to Ian, the stick is better.

On it goes, the sounds drifting into my pine-scented cave through the branches of the mighty tree in which I'm engulfed. Kaylee tromps beside me in a happy silence, rain-booted feet, mittened hands, face glowing with the cold.

Home to hot chocolate, and a Christmas beer for me.

The tree looms large in our family room; they always look so much smaller outside. Father Christmas is perched at the top, the lights are on, and it's time for the ornaments. I love decorating the tree, digging into the boxes of carefully wrapped ornaments with the tissue paper rustling like the winter-dried grasses of the tree farm. I love listening to Ian and Kaylee talk about certain ornaments that are special to them.

"Look, Ian, you made this one in kindergarten," Kaylee says.

"This one is from Disneyland."

"I made that one in preschool!"

I always pause when I come to two identical plastic candy canes. These plain, simple ornaments are from a wonderful weekend that started out horribly.

Each year, a few days before Christmas, my parents take us all to a fancy hotel on the coast for two nights as our Christmas present. The place is a beautiful old Victorian, which Kaylee and Ian call "The Christmas Hotel." The owners never seem to have the reservations quite right, and the water in the shower turns suddenly cold with no warning; but the huge, wonderfully decorated tree in the lobby, the Christmas ornament on our pillow, the massive stone fireplace that is always lit, and years of memories make up for that.

On the first night, we have dinner together in the hotel's five-star dining room. It's a long, drawn-out affair with too much of everything—too much rich food, too much wine, too much conversation—the food tends to get cold. It's absolutely wonderful.

It was the year Ian turned two; our last Christmas before Kaylee was born.

Michelle and I got a late start; it was beginning to rain, and packing the car took longer than we had planned. When we finally left the house, the roads were horrible and drenched with rain like I'd never seen. We called ahead to let the rest of my family know that we wouldn't make it in time for dinner. During the entire drive, all I could think of was the restaurant—my family's faces in the candlelight, the food, the wine. We arrived just as they were coming out of the restaurant.

"Are you guys okay?" Mom asked. She could see by my face how disappointed I was.

"The roads were awful. I'm just glad we're here."

"Let's get up to our room," Michelle said. "Ian's had it."

In the elevator I realized we hadn't even looked at the tree in the lobby.

"Tomorrow will be better," I said to myself as I unlocked the door to our room. On our pillow was a simple candy-cane ornament.

Ian was up all night, and the next morning he was inconsolable.

"We should just go home," I said. "We're wasting Mom and Dad's money staying here with Ian like this."

Michelle agreed and we left later that morning; we were sad and exhausted. The drive home was worse than the day before. The windshield wipers couldn't keep up with the downpour. We literally crept along the road. We were halfway home when we came to a roadblock. A highway patrolman stood there in the rain.

"The road's closed. There's been a huge slide ahead. I have no idea when they'll clear it. You guys should head back where you came from."

We stopped at the first pay phone we came to and called Mom and Dad's room.

"I'll see if I can get you another room," Dad said. "I don't know though. They're pretty full."

There was nothing more we could do; we drove on with our fingers crossed. Dad was waiting in the lobby when we arrived with a key in his hand. I can't begin to describe our relief.

This time we stopped to look at the tree. It was beautiful. We sat on the hearth before the fire. Ian was calm and happily chattering about the tree. I looked at him with the lights from the tree shining in his eyes. The fire crackled and popped, its heat soaking through my shirt as the rain continued to pour down outside—I felt like we were home.

"Let's go unpack," Michelle said.

As I unlocked the door to our room, I thought back on the previous night, remembering how exhausted and disappointed we'd been. I laid our suitcase on the bed, and there it was . . . another candy-cane ornament on the pillow, beautiful in its simplicity.

There was a soft knock on the door. Mom stood in the hall.

"Go down and get some dinner," she said. "I'll watch Ian."

The waiter led us past the large table in the center of the room where we usually sat with the rest of the family. A large group was sitting there, much like my own family, boisterously loud in their camaraderie. We were led to a table for two in a quiet corner of the warm, oak-paneled room. I gazed across the table at Michelle's beautiful face, glowing in the candlelight, poured her a glass of wine, and raised my own in a quiet toast.

"Merry Christmas."

I've rarely meant it more.

{ 67 }

New Year's Eve

"Ten, nine, eight…"

We huddled together on the patio in the cold moonlight, counting away the last seconds of 2003. Ian and Kaylee were poised and ready; a metal pot and spoon clutched tightly in their hands.

"Three, two, ONE, ZERO! Happy New Year!"

Ian and Kaylee let loose on their pans, the sharp metal clangs floating off into the misty midnight air.

"Happy New Year, Sweets," I said to Michelle, clinking my glass of champagne against hers.

"Happy New Year," she said, shivering as she gave me a quick kiss. "I'm going inside, I'm freezing."

Ian and Kaylee went in with her, and I was left alone with the deep silence and the clear light of the stars.

To me, there is something awesome about New Year's Eve. Time seems to slow, and I can almost feel this old Earth as it slowly spins out the last moments of the year.

I turned and looked into the house. Our Christmas tree stood there in the bay window, and through its branches I could see my family sitting together on the couch, their faces glowing in the light from the tree.

"Your whole world is sitting in there," I said to myself quietly.

And with those words, my mind raced back to another New Year's Eve, a beautiful night like this one, fourteen years ago. The New Year's Eve where it all started.

Michelle and I walked through the grass of the field, moving up the hill to the top where the view is best. It was a cold, clear winter night, and it all lay there before us: the beautiful mountain that seems to grow right from the lake, a scarf of mist wrapped around its mighty shoulder; the stars bright and sharp, like diamonds of light; the cold night air, its candy-cane breath in our lungs. All was silent but for the call of a heron, mournful and beautiful. It was New Year's Eve and the world was hushed, readying itself for the coming year.

We stood quietly together at the top of the field and gazed out at the lake, and the mountain, and the stars. Michelle's hand was warm in my own.

Then from far off we heard the first sounds greeting the New Year—shouts and firecrackers broke the silence. I thought of those hot, sweaty rooms, the music and the noise; the faces flushed with drink. Here was better.

I gripped Michelle's hand a little tighter, waiting for the sounds to die away. Silence then, and the night once again belonged to the mountain, the stars . . . and to us.

"Will you marry me?" I asked.

"Okay." She was crying, warm breath a mist in the air.

I stood there on the patio for a long time, thinking of that night fourteen years ago when my world changed forever. The midnight stars spun slowly above my head, and the Earth spun beneath my feet.

There is a Buddhist saying that I like: "Look for gifts." I raised my glass in silent toast and drained it. My gifts were waiting for me inside.

{ 68 }

A Battered Door

A scream of frustration and the crash of a door shatter the quiet of the house. It draws us to Ian's room. He's slammed and locked the door, but after years of this, the jam is in splinters, and it is easily opened.

We find . . . not Ian, but that hateful animal hiding beneath Ian's flesh, an animal that takes over that beautiful body and uses it to hurt and destroy.

I move in quickly and pull him to the ground as he lashes out at me. Michelle comes in behind to grab his legs as he begins to kick. We settle in and, as so often before, ride out the storm.

And then it's over. Ian has returned more quickly than ever before. The three of us stand up in awkward surprise and return in silent wonder to what we were doing before.

His battered door swings there in its shattered frame and waits for the next time.

{ 69 }

Questions and Answers

"**A**re you okay?" I asked.

Kaylee sat on the floor of her room with a book on her lap, but she wasn't reading.

"Yes, Daddy."

"No you're not."

"I am . . . really."

"I can tell you're not," I said.

"How do you know?"

" 'Cuz Dads know everything," I said, sitting down and pulling her into my lap.

We'd had to restrain Ian again, and the awful words he'd screamed at us still hung in the air.

Kaylee was quiet, her blonde head leaning against my chest.

"Are you thinking about Ian?" I asked.

"Kind of…"

"Tell me."

"I don't like it when he screams."

"Neither do I."

"Does it hurt him when you hold him down?"

"No, Kaylee. It might sound like it, but it doesn't."

"I hate it that Ian has autism."

My heart sank.

"Oh, Baby Girl." I hugged her close and stroked her hair as I searched for words to say.

"You know something?" I asked.

"What."

"Ian wouldn't be Ian if he didn't have autism. As hard as it is, like tonight, Ian's autism has some pretty cool parts to it."

"Tonight it didn't."

"You're right. Tonight was a hard night. But it's not always like this, and he's getting better."

"You mean it'll go away?"

"No, it'll never go away. Ian will always have autism. I wouldn't want it to go away," I added.

"Why?"

"Because then he wouldn't be Ian. You want to know something else?"

"What."

"Living with Ian is helping you grow into a wonderfully caring and accepting person. The world needs more people like that."

I gave her a kiss on the top of her head and left her with those words.

{ 70 }

Wednesday

The longest Wednesday of my life began a few weeks before Thanksgiving. I look back on it now and laugh, but living that day was awful.

Ian has the constitution of an ox. On that Wednesday, Michelle, Kaylee, and I had the worst case of the flu—I discovered aching joints I never knew I had—but Ian weathered the weeklong storm with nary a sniffle. It began on a Sunday night. We were driving back home from a visit to Michelle's parents, a two-hour drive, and by the time we arrived, Michelle and I were feeling awful.

Frequently Ian will get a topic stuck in his head. It could be anything; currently it's mountain lions. The thoughts whirl round and round in there, and he drives us all crazy asking the same questions over and over again. When I'm really sick, a similar thing happens to me. It's something that only a fellow musician, or perhaps an autistic, can appreciate. A song will get stuck in my head, running away in an infinite loop—over and over and over. It wouldn't be quite so bad if it were the whole song. My problem is that only part of the song gets stuck, and it always cuts off and repeats in the middle of a measure. For example, if the tune were "Mary Had A Little Lamb," it would sound something like this:

"Mary had a lit . . . Mary had a lit . . . Mary had a lit . . ." over and over. It's truly maddening.

When Michelle gets up in the morning, she puts music on in the kids' rooms to wake them up. She varies the music. The week we were sick, she chose a piece of music that I had written for Ian when he was born. The first day it was kind of nice to hear it drifting into our room. I think the fever helped me listen to the music without criticizing it like I usually do and I was actually enjoying it. Then the inevitable happened, and Ian's song became a loop in my head. It's an instrumental piece, and the point it began to loop was right on this certain note that I've never been totally satisfied with. I think I hate that song now, and after having that bum note drilled into my head something like nine million times, I know I'm going to have to re-record it.

"Blum de dum dum . . . blum de dum dum . . . Mary had a lit, Mary had a lit . . ." It was horrible.

Michelle had been far too sick to do the laundry, and as a result it hadn't been done in days. I couldn't have helped even if I'd been able to. One of the smartest things I've ever done in my life was to turn all of our underwear pink early in our relationship. I've not been allowed in the laundry room since.

Late on Tuesday night, a need to bathe broke through my delirium. I had a strange idea that I could wash away the plague that was raging through my body. After my shower I staggered to my dresser for a pair of underwear; there were none. It seemed quite logical to my fevered brain to put on a pair of Michelle's; the woman has enough underwear to clothe an army. I chose a pink, flowered pair—French cut I believe—and crawled back into bed.

Wednesday arrived, and to my amazement Michelle climbed out of bed and got dressed for work. Getting her to take care of herself when she's sick is a battle of wills, which I generally lose. Kaylee was ready to go back to school, and I guess Michelle thought it would just be easier to go as well.

I had just drifted back to sleep when the screaming started. I leaped out of bed. For a moment, I thought perhaps I'd dreamed it; I stood there in the middle of the room, swaying slightly, and tried to get my bearings. The screams continued. They sounded horrible, and they were coming from the driveway.

I ran for the front door. Michelle was coming back in as I pushed past her, trying to get outside. She grabbed me and pulled me back towards the house. I could see Ian in the car, mouth wide, wailing like a wild thing. I fought to free myself from Michelle's grip. I couldn't understand why she was trying to get me back in the house.

"Get inside!" she yelled over the din.

"What's wrong with Ian? I need to get to the car!"

"Then put your robe on!" Michelle said.

It was then that I noticed the cold and realized that I was standing in the middle of the driveway wearing nothing but Michelle's underwear.

It turned out that Ian had managed to get his finger stuck in the cat carrier. Kaylee was bringing the cat to school for sharing. We finally freed Ian's finger, and Michelle got me back to bed. As I lay there dozing, I had an image of our neighbor calling for help.

"This is 911. What is your emergency?"

"There's a man running around my neighbor's car. He's wearing women's underwear. The kids are screaming inside . . . please send the police!"

I told Michelle that I'd pick the kids up that day. It was parent conference week, and the kids were on half days. I'd set the alarm for 11:30 to give myself plenty of time so I could drive the back way . . . slowly. As I look back on it, it wasn't my best decision. I could barely stand up, yet I expected to be able to drive?

I walked slowly to the car, got in, waited for the world to quit spinning, and then started the engine. I backed slowly down the driveway. Everything seemed to be fine until I realized that the car wasn't moving. I looked at the dashboard, there were no weird red lights. I could hear the engine going. I looked in the rearview mirror.

"I don't remember that tree being there," I said to myself.

I pressed the gas pedal again. There was a strange spinning sound.

"Sounds like the wheels."

I got out and saw that I'd backed off the driveway and was stuck in a huge pile of leaves.

I hoped the neighbors weren't home as I stood there digging my car out.

"At least I've got my pants on this time," I said to myself as I drove on my way.

That night Michelle was feeling sick again after working all day, so I sent her to bed. I managed to get the kids fed—a slow process since I had to keep sitting down every few minutes. Finally it was bedtime. We were in the kitchen, and I decided to give Kaylee some cough medicine for her lingering cold. She took one sip, gagged, and promptly threw up on my legs. It is putting it mildly to say that I cannot stand the sight, sound, or smell of vomit. Ian is worse than me. As I stood there horrified, Ian made a kind of animal-like shriek and fled. Kaylee looked as if more was coming.

"Quick, into the bathroom!" I gasped in-between dry heaves.

Kaylee barely made it in the door before she blasted the bathroom floor. She began to cry.

"Come here, baby girl," I said, trying to sound calm as my stomach was heaving.

"Why don't you get in a nice warm shower and get yourself cleaned up."

I had no idea where Ian was, but I could hear him.

"I'm trapped!"

"What?"

"I'm trapped!" he wailed.

"Ian it's okay, I'll get this cleaned up. You stay where you are. I'll come when I'm done."

"I can't go in my room. There's Kaylee's throw up. I can't sleep in my bed!"

I wanted to wake Michelle with every single fiber of my being. I kill the spiders; she deals with the barf. That's the way it had always been, and life until that moment had been wonderful. But as I stood there with vomit dripping down my leg, I couldn't bring myself to drag her from bed. It took me about thirty minutes to get it all cleaned up. As it turned out, I woke her with the sounds of my retching anyway.

I tucked Kaylee into bed with a bucket beside her and then turned my attention to Ian. I hadn't heard him for a while, and I thought that perhaps he'd gone to bed on his own. I found him on the couch with his head buried under the cushions.

"I thought maybe you'd gone to bed," I said.

"I can't, I'm trapped."

"What do you mean 'you're trapped'?" I asked.

"I can't get into my room!" he moaned.

"It's okay, I cleaned it all up."

"But I can smell it."

I don't know if it's part of his autism, but Ian has always been extremely sensitive to smells. It took half a can of air freshener to get him into bed.

The world was beginning to spin again, and I could tell I was running a fever. I took a couple of aspirin and climbed wearily into bed. The longest Wednesday of my entire life was finally dragging itself to a close. Michelle felt warm and soft at my side; her breathing was gentle and even. I sighed, closed my eyes, and then it started.

"Mary had a lit . . . Mary had a lit . . . Mary had a lit . . . "

Sometimes life just sucks.

{ 71 }

Rough

"This is my dad. His name is Hank. We play 'Rough' on weekends, and at the end we do push down. I always win because I'm strong."

An interesting way to be introduced to a complete stranger, but over the years I've gotten used to it. Sometimes I feel that in Ian's mind, all that I am good for is weekend evenings spent roughhousing.

It all began with a green plastic pickup truck.

Ian was two when Kaylee was born. We were still in denial mode, pretending that all was well. We wanted to believe that his severe expressive and receptive language delays were normal and that they would work themselves out as he got older. We still thought his obsession with the dryer and the vacuum cleaner were cute eccentricities, and that his tantrums were still a part of the "terrible two's."

Friends had been coming by in a steady stream to see Kaylee. She was a wonderful week-old, dark-haired bundle of "new baby smell."

"This is for you, Ian," a friend from school said, handing him a brightly wrapped package.

Nearly every visitor remembered to include Ian, and he had quite an assortment of new toys and stuffed animals collecting in his room. Most of them were untouched since being unwrapped. Even at two, his interests were obsessive and narrow.

Ian clapped with delight and tore off the colorful paper to reveal a large, green plastic pickup truck.

"What do you say, Bug?" Michelle asked.

"Nk oo!"

"You're welcome sweetie. Now let's see your new sister."

Soon the green truck was sitting with the other toys in his bedroom . . . forgotten.

A few days later I was walking by his room and saw the truck sitting there. Ian had never shown much interest in cars and trucks, and we were forever trying to broaden his interests. I could see Ian standing in the kitchen, so I got the truck and rolled it towards him. It bumped into his leg.

"BRRRRCH!" I said, making a car crash sound.

Ian laughed and rolled it back.

I stood up and brought the truck into the living room.

"Ian, go stand by your bedroom door."

I sat down on the floor and rolled the truck towards him. It shot through the kitchen, into the hallway, and crashed into his leg.

"BRRRCH!" we said together.

Ian laughed and rolled it back. We spent a long time simply rolling the truck back and forth. It felt so good to play with him, to interact with him as I would with any two-year-old boy . . . a rare event in our lives.

It was my turn to roll the truck when it veered to the side and crashed into the kitchen counter. Ian laughed in delight and came running to get it. I grabbed him, tackled him to the floor and tickled him.

"Gin, gin!" he screeched.

"You want to do it again? Go back to your door!"

This time I intentionally crashed the truck. Ian came charging out of his room and smashed into me. We rolled on the floor laughing.

"Gin, gin, gin!" Ian yelled.

. . . and so the game of "Rough" was born.

Somehow, along the way, a stepladder was added to the mix. After the crash, Ian would climb the ladder, and I would pull him to the floor. As Kaylee got older and began to crawl, she would be in the thick of it, smashed in the pile. We would finish—battered, bruised sometimes— happy, sweaty, and exhausted.

Ian is eleven now, Kaylee almost nine, and we still play "Rough." The game has been relegated to weekend evenings, and over the years it has evolved.

"So . . . do you want to play "Rough"?"

Ian has a wonderful way of tearing into the word rough—pirate-like in its intensity. "Rough" has been reduced into a choice of two games, and Ian and Kaylee take turns choosing which to play.

Kaylee always chooses "Hide and Seek Rough." One of us hides, while the other two count in Michelle's and my bedroom. When I'm counting, Ian or Kaylee tries to escape, and I tackle them and throw them on the bed. Our bedroom is usually trashed by the end.

Ian chooses "Fight Rough," which is played in the living room. The game is simple . . . Ian and Kaylee attack me, and I try to fight them off. During the game, couch pillows are thrown everywhere, lamps get knocked over, and one of us invariably gets hurt. We love it. There is a certain CD of mine that Ian likes to have playing loudly, and through it all the dogs bark hysterically.

Michelle is usually finishing up the dinner dishes during "Rough" and therefore safe from the chaos. For years Ian and Kaylee were so focused on pummeling me that Michelle was largely ignored . . . that changed a few years ago.

"Let's get Mommy," Ian whispered.

"Yeah, let's get her!" Kaylee agreed.

It sounded like a good idea to me. There she was, safe in the kitchen while I was being beaten to a pulp. We snuck up behind

Michelle while she stood at the sink and, screaming maniacally, dragged her to the floor to tickle her.

She expects it now, but she still plays along, feigning surprise as she is attacked with screams of "GET MOMMY!"

The woman has been tickled, tied up with jump ropes, and had ice put down her back. Usually we finish her off by dragging her outside . . . rain or shine. The kids and I agree, rain is best. One time we burst screaming into the kitchen only to find her gone. We tore the house apart looking for her, but she had vanished.

"Where's Mommy?" Kaylee asked.

"Maybe she's hiding outside," Ian said.

"I doubt it, it's raining," I said, "let's go look just in case."

There she was, sitting in the car, reading a book with a flashlight. Of course she had the doors locked. She just sat there laughing while Ian and Kaylee ran from door to door screaming as loud as they could.

I sometimes wonder what the neighbors must think.

***

"GET MOMMY!" we screamed.

Michelle fought back like a wild woman, but we soon overwhelmed her and dragged her to the door. It was a winter night, cold and wet, perfect "Get Mommy" weather.

"NO!" she yelled, as Kaylee opened the front door.

The dogs were barking happily. The kids were yelling and laughing. Michelle was screaming.

The police will be arriving any minute, I thought to myself.

As we got her outside, the door suddenly slammed and I heard the click of the lock. I found myself standing there in a cold rain with Michelle at my side. Ian and Kaylee leered at us through the closed door.

"You realize they have us completely under their control,"

Michelle said.

"I love Saturdays," I said as I kissed her.

{ 72 }

Fathers and Sons

I sat there on the floor and watched Ian open his birthday presents. My dad was sitting behind me on the couch, and he began to rub my back as he so often does—as he has done for the past forty-two years. He's got this habit; he passes behind you, stops, kind of absently rubs your back for a bit, and then moves on. No words are spoken; there's just the connection, which is probably more important. I do the same with my own children. I guess I got it from him.

As I leaned back and watched my twelve-year-old son, I was struck by a sudden thought, *God, Dad's almost eighty.*

He'd missed Ian's last birthday. His lung had collapsed while he was out working in the yard, and he'd been recovering from the surgery.

"Is Grandpa going to die?" Ian had asked when I told him Grandpa couldn't come to his party.

"No, Ian, but Grandpa is having a big operation to make him better, and it'll take a long time for him to feel strong again."

Ian seemed content with my answer, but I felt uneasy. I'd never really thought about Dad dying before.

I looked around my house. I'd done a lot of remodeling over the years, most of it with Dad by my side. We'd joke with one another about how much we bled during our work. We were forever cutting or scraping ourselves without realizing it until we'd see a blood smear. I laughed when I tore up the linoleum in the kid's bathroom last year and found bloodstains on the subfloor that Dad and I had replaced years ago. Dad's blood or mine, or perhaps both, mingled there forever, staining the wood. I like that. My father and I have been through a lot together, times when we were close, and times when we were far apart. We are close now, closer than ever, for now we are friends.

I wondered, as I sat watching my son, if Dad was thinking of a similar time. A birthday now long past when he watched me as I opened my gifts. His son, safe, happy, content, and dependent on him for everything. That boy is a man now, with a family of his own, and busy finding his own way through life. I hope he is proud of me.

Ian yelled with excitement over one of his gifts. I settled back into that "Dad smell" I know and love, and wondered:

Where will I be when Ian is forty-two? Will he be on his own? Will there be a similar party, with Ian sitting as I sit now, watching his own son? One day will he find our blood mingled together on a floor or wall of his home?

Sometimes I think the answers will be no, and I am saddened by that.

{ 73 }

Thoughts

My head felt thick, my heart was flailing away in my chest, and I was exhausted. Ian, calm now, was easing off into an uneasy sleep, alone in the dark with remnants of his rage.

I fell into my chair. The house was quiet but for the faraway sounds of Ian and Kaylee's lullaby tapes murmuring in the background and the heavy breathing of the dogs at my feet; familiar, comforting sounds made hollow in the aftermath of the violence and the noise. Michelle was gone for the evening teaching her dance class.

I was alone, as only the parent of an autistic can be. Alone with the horrible words he'd said. Alone with the pain from where the slamming door had caught my shoulder. Alone with the memory of those eyes that for a moment looked at me with hate, and alone with my fears for the future.

I sat there for a long time, trying to find some semblance of calm, but peace was far out of my reach.

Why is this one such a big deal? I thought. *It's no different from any of the others.*

And then I had it. The reason this one had hit me so hard was that it had been a long time since the last rage. I sat there trying to remember the last time, and couldn't.

I'm out of practice, I laughed to myself.

Suddenly my thoughts froze and focused on what I'd almost let slip by.

You can't remember when his last rage was, I said to myself. *Has it really been that long?*

The sounds of the lullabies drifted out to me, sweet and soft. A dog sighed and shifted his warm body closer to my leg. I leaned back deep into my chair and let the portent of those words drift over me.

I can't remember Ian's last rage.

Slumber Parties

Kaylee is a very popular girl. Her "social calendar" tends to fill up very quickly. There always seems to be a birthday party, play date, or sleepover looming on the horizon. I choose the word looming because of Ian.

The only birthday parties Ian is invited to are for cousins and close family friends. The only place he's ever gone for a sleepover is Anna's, Michelle's job-sharing partner. When he was younger, he never seemed to notice how often Kaylee was away. Michelle and I always tried to make those evenings extra special for him: a favorite dinner, a special movie from the video store, an extra wild game of Rough. Sadly, though, as he gets older our efforts to distract him aren't working as well. He's beginning to feel left out.

***

He sits there watching Kaylee wrap a birthday present for a friend.

"You're going to a birthday party, huh?"

"Yes, Ian!" Kaylee sounds frustrated. he's asked that question four times already.

"It's just for girls, huh?"

"Yes, Ian!"

"No boys allowed . . . "

"You know the answer!"

He's asking about the girls to reassure himself and to make sure he's not being excluded once again. Invariably he'll soon turn to me.

"I jumped on the trampoline at Skylar's party."

"Yep, you sure did," I say.

"I was the good guy. I protected the girls."

"You had fun, didn't you?"

"If a bad guy really came, I'd fight him off, and . . . "

The words will go on and on, always the same. He is speaking of a party that happened two years ago, a party to which he was not invited. It was a birthday slumber party for a friend of Kaylee's. Ian and I went to pick Kaylee up, and I got to talking with the little girl's mother. I was there much longer than I expected, and when I was finally ready to leave, Ian and the girls were involved in a wild game on the trampoline. I stood there watching. They were screaming and laughing with Ian at the center of attention.

"He's such a great kid." The girl's mother had come up beside me.

"He's come a long way. I love to see him playing like this," I said.

He talks about that party every time Kaylee is invited to go somewhere. In his mind, he feels like he was invited. As far as I know, he's got it worked out that he was there the whole time.

I can almost see his face glowing in the light of the birthday candles—the momentary uncertainty at bedtime when he realizes we are not with him—before he snuggles down in his sleeping bag and falls asleep.

I choose to let him believe what he wants.

{ 75 }

Family Night

One Thursday night a month, they have a Family Night at Ian and Kaylee's school. Each month focuses on a different academic subject. Last night was Family Science Night.

Kaylee turned to her brother. "Ian, do you want to go to Family Science Night tomorrow? There will be lots of games and snacks, and you'll get a homework pass."

It was Wednesday night. We were sitting at the dinner table, and Kaylee was excited. My daughter is a very social creature. She's only nine, but she has already discovered the joys of talking for hours on the phone. She loves Family Nights. The moment we step into the school cafeteria, she's off and soon surrounded by her group of friends.

Ian seemed doubtful. "Will I miss my cartoons?"

"You'll be able to see most of them," I said, hoping to convince him. Ian is very set in his routines; always hesitant to try anything new. "It'll be fun, Ian."

"There are prizes!" Kaylee said.

That did it.

"Okay," he said. "Mom, are you coming?"

"No, Ian. I've got my dance class."

Michelle teaches her class on Thursdays, and as a result I've seen her maybe four Thursday nights in fifteen years of marriage.

"You might win a prize, Ian, or maybe not . . . everyone won't get one," she added.

"Don't go just for a prize. There's a good chance you won't win," I said. I could just see him throwing a fit if he lost.

"I'll go," he said.

"Remember, you might not win," Michelle said again.

"I know, stop telling me that."

By Thursday afternoon, the reality of missing some of his cartoons and his other Thursday rituals was beginning to sink in.

"I don't want to go to Science Night."

"Ian, it's too late to change your mind. I don't have anyone to stay with you," I said.

"You could leave me."

We had started leaving him home alone for very quick runs to the market. We were up to around 20 minutes.

"That's too long to be alone, Ian. Come with us, you'll have fun."

"And there'll be prizes!" Kaylee said, a note of panic in her voice. I could almost see her visions of "Social Night 2004" dissolving before her eyes.

"You *might* win a prize," I added hastily.

"Yea, you *might* win, but you might not." Kaylee obviously had caught on to the idea. "You can't get mad."

"Sometimes I win, sometimes I don't," Ian said, ever the philosopher.

By the time we arrived, the cafeteria was packed. Kaylee instantly disappeared. I didn't see her again for an hour. I stuck by Ian.

"How do I get a prize?"

"Remember, Ian, there are lots of kids here; you probably won't win. You need to go see Mrs. Ferguson. She'll have you write your name on a ticket for the drawing."

Ian went off to find her, and I followed behind.

"Mrs. Ferguson, can I have a ticket?"

"Remember, Ian, you might not win." She knows Ian too well. I'm sure he imagined some vast conspiracy against him.

"I know, my dad said."

. . . and my mom, and my sister, and my mom again, and my dad again, and my sister . . . I imagined him adding.

Ian had fun. He went to each table, and I was struck again, as I always am, at how kind and patient everyone is with him . . . and not just the teachers, but the kids and parents as well. As always, he was unfailingly polite and charming. He left many a smiling face in his wake.

"It's time for the drawing!" Mrs. Ferguson stood on a table. The kids gathered around.

I nearly grabbed Ian on his way to remind him about the prizes, but I caught myself.

Let him be, I thought.

Ian was toward the front, eyes glued on Mrs. Ferguson. Kaylee suddenly reappeared and sat next to him. They usually draw ten tickets, and as Mrs. Ferguson began to read off the names, it grew quiet—all except for Ian.

Each name was followed by a comment from Ian. "Good job!" "Yay!" "Way to go!" "She's in my class!"

I looked at him and smiled. Sometimes he makes me so proud.

"We've got five prizes left," Mrs. Ferguson announced.

I looked at Ian to make sure he was still okay. He had his hand over his head, five fingers up.

" . . . and number five is, Lisa!"

"Yea, Lisa!" Ian called happily. One finger went down, four remained.

"Number four is . . . Bobby!"

"I know Bobby!" Three fingers left.

"And the next lucky winner . . . IAN!"

Ian jumped into the air with his hand raised in a thumbs up.

"That's me!" he cried.

People were cheering. They hadn't cheered for the other kids, but they were cheering for Ian. Maybe I'm being dramatic, but looking around, I felt as though everyone was smiling as Ian went up to the table to choose his prize.

As we were driving home, Ian said, "I won a prize Dad, huh?"

"Yep, you sure did."

"Not all the kids won."

"You're right, some kids didn't get picked."

"I got picked, but I would be okay if I didn't get picked, huh?"

"You would have been a good sport."

He paused for a minute. "They clapped for me, huh?"

"Yes, they did."

"People didn't clap for the others. Why did they clap for me?"

Images from the evening passed through my mind. Ian so happy and excited at each table, and so polite. Ian standing there rooting for the other kids during the drawing with his fingers over his head counting down the last five. His excitement at winning, so genuine, and the people smiling at him as he chose his prize.

"You must be a pretty special kid, Ian," I said.

{ 76 }

A Quiet Evening

"You forgot to tape my cartoons?" Ian cried, his voice beginning to rise.

We stood by the front door and faced off like boxers. Michelle stood nearby, tense and ready. We were at the end of a long week, and had been looking forward to a quiet evening.

"Ian, you've got to remind me after breakfast. It gets so crazy in the morning that I forget . . . you know that."

God, no rage tonight . . . I can't face it, I thought to myself.

We stood there, poised on the brink. On the one side a quiet, gentle evening after a long hard day. On the other, chaos and violence. And after, exhaustion and a cold bitter silence, which were almost worse.

Ian took a deep breath, let it out slowly, and said, "Well, that's okay. I'll go play my game."

Michelle and I stood there looking at each other.

"I don't believe it," she said quietly.

Our evening had just been delivered to us on the quiet breath of our son.

Orc Feet

I suppressed a scream of pain as Michelle dragged her bare foot down my leg. There's nothing quite like being ripped from a sound sleep by a swipe from one of Michelle's feet. They have to be seen to be believed. They look okay from a distance, but up close you notice the firewalker calluses and the general aura of abuse. To be polite, I suppose one might call them "dancer's feet", I call them "orc feet."

I still bear the scar on my arm from the time Michelle learned what that meant. We were sitting in the movie theater watching *The Lord of the Rings*. I try not to think about it, but the memory of her flashing brown eyes and her fingernails burrowing into the flesh of my arm still haunts me.

Michelle teaches clogging, which is a combination of Irish, tap, and God knows what else. The years of abuse show in her feet, and she is passing it on to my children.

Ian and Kaylee have been dancing with Michelle since they were old enough to walk, indeed since they were in the womb. I have horrible memories of Michelle, extremely pregnant with Kaylee, dancing in 100 degree heat at the Lake County Fair. She got so hot that the people manning the nearby beer stand made her lie down in the back of their refrigerated truck. After being battered around for nearly an hour, my future daughter finished off the day with a healthy dose of beer fumes.

Watching Kaylee dance is wonderful. She is a natural, graceful and confident. Ian is fun to watch too, but for very different reasons.

There is no denying the fact that Ian brings his own "style" to clogging. Ian approaches clogging with stage-shaking exuberance. His face is a picture of concentration. He loves a step called "unclog"— step step, drag . . . step step, drag—he careens his way to the front of the stage as the younger dancers dive from his path. The eternal showman, he nods his head and smiles to the adoring crowd before he unclogs his way to the back again—step step, drag . . . step step, drag—the other dancers part before him like the Red Sea. But Ian's favorite part of any clogging show has nothing to do with dancing.

"We're special, huh?" Ian said as we drove to yet another show.

"I think you're special, Bug," I said.

"No, I mean 'cuz of Mom."

"Huh?"

"Because me and Kaylee are Mom's kids."

"Oh, and she's the teacher of the class."

"Yea, and she introduces me. She says, 'My son, Ian.'"

At the end of every show, Michelle introduces each dancer, and she always introduces Ian and Kaylee as her children. When she mentions Ian, he literally swells with pride—chest jutting out and head held high.

As this show ended, Michelle began to introduce her tired dancers. I could see Ian's face light up in anticipation.

"And in the second row, Rebecca, Sara, Ian, Lisa . . . "

Oh my God, she forgot to say Ian was her son! I thought in horror.

I looked for Ian in the line. He looked as though he was going to cry.

"In the front we have Terrie, my daughter Kaylee, Tanya . . . " Michelle paused. "I forgot to say Ian was my son! Ian wave to everyone."

Ian leapt to the front of the stage, scattering two unfortunate five-year-olds in the process. The day was saved.

Michelle runs two different dance teams, an adult group and a kid's group. In April, Michelle and her adults dance in a big local dance festival. For that month, I learn what it must be like to be a single father.

"Where's Mom?" Ian asks. He knows full well what she's doing. I think he enjoys the wistful look I get when I think about "ol' What's Her Name."

"Where do you think Mommy is?"

"Dancing, huh? She's dancing, right?"

"Yes, Ian. You knew the answer though, didn't you?"

"Where's Kaylee?"

"Where is Kaylee, Ian?"

"At Rebecca's birthday party." He pauses. "Can we play "Rough" tonight?"

"Ian, tonight is hard, it's just Daddy tonight."

"Mom's dancing, huh?"

"You know the answer."

"Can we play squirt fight?"

"Ian, it's dark out, plus it's too cold, plus I've got the dishes to do. Remember, it's just me tonight."

"Ah man!" he says.

I look at the dishes piled in the sink. Feeling weariness in my bones, I look longingly at my chair. It beckons to me with the promise of music, a good book, and perhaps as glass of wine —or three—but the house is trashed and we have Michelle's mom coming tomorrow to watch Michelle in the Dance Festival. My chair image pops like a balloon.

"Please? It's not a school night," Ian begs.

"It's too dark, Ian."

"How about Rough?"

"No, Bug." I turn to the dishes. "Maybe tomorrow."

"Okay." He sighs and wanders off.

The pile of dishes seems larger than before. I turn on the hot water, add some soap and wait as the sink fills. Ian's soulful eyes float before me in the warm, soap-scented fog. I turn off the water and go to find him.

"So," I say in my best roguish voice, "do you wanna play "Rough"?"

Kaylee returns from her party in the middle of the game and happily joins in. The three of us batter each other silly, and by the end, the house is in an even worse state than before. The dishes remain in the sink, untouched. But the kids go to bed happy, and so do I. I read one or two sentences in my book before I fall asleep.

Michelle returns at some god-forsaken hour, and I'm vaguely aware as she climbs into bed beside me. With one last convulsive shudder, the last bit of energy leaves her body, and she's asleep.

"I love you," I whisper as I pull her close.

"Rrrgmmfff," she replies.

I smile and close my eyes, slowly drifting away… and then those damn feet find me again.

78

Armpits and Weddings

"Anna, watch!" Ian yelled.

He stood on the driveway next to Anna's car, left hand under his armpit, right arm working like a piston. His face was contorted in delighted concentration as he produced a series of rude sounds.

Anna, Michelle's job-share partner, was in her car preparing to leave after dropping off Michelle's lesson plan book. I watched as her blonde head sank slowly to the seat in hysterics.

"Ian, you need to stop so Anna can leave," I said laughing.

He ignored me and continued his gyrations with the dedication of a pro.

"Blame your husband!" I called to Anna's tear-streamed face. "He's the one who taught him that."

Ian was fixated on his armpit for the next few months, but gradually the interest waned, much to our relief. By June, I had forgotten all about it.

We were at the wedding of a friend's daughter. It was outdoors, and the narrow rectangle of newly-laid sod was packed with rows and rows of plastic white chairs. It was hot, and the fortunate few who had arrived early were packed into the shade of a large oak tree. We never arrive early for anything, so we sat, slowly roasting in the sun. Anna and her boys, Matt and Mark, had shown up when we did, so we sat together, adults in the front, the kids in the row behind.

Ian was glad to see Matt, and soon they were chattering happily about video games.

"Where're Steve and Molly? How'd he manage to get out of this?" I asked, wiping sweat from my forehead.

"He should be along. They're at Molly's baseball game."

As Anna was speaking, Steve and their daughter Molly wandered up. Steve was resplendent in a shirt covered with pineapples.

"Nice shirt," I said, reaching to shake his hand.

"Hey, it's my Father's Day present," he said smiling. "Hi, Ian!"

"Hey, Steve!"

Suddenly it got quiet, and I could see the wedding party lining up. I pitied the men in their tuxedos.

"Hey, Steve, want to see me make a farting noise with my knee?" Ian bawled into the silence.

He's sitting behind us, maybe no one will know he's ours, I thought as I sank lower in my chair.

Mercifully, Pachelbel's Canon started up, and all eyes were on the bride.

I've listened to Pachelbel's Canon many times over the years, but I had to admit as I sat there in the hot August sun that knee farts were an interesting addition.

79

Wine and Avocados

I remember another wedding, many years earlier. Michelle was on the dance floor dancing with no one in particular—fluid, beautiful, carefree. Ian and I had a quiet corner to ourselves. A bottle of wine was at my elbow and I was feeding him avocados. His first solid food, a rather momentous occasion for a new parent. I suppose it should have been a moment of excited phone calls to the grandparents along with the flash of the camera, but Ian and I were alone and quiet. I remember a feeling of complete contentment and well-being as I sipped my wine and Ian gummed his avocados.

Ian used to stand at our back fence and toss rocks into the brush on the other side. There was an old piece of metal rain gutter over there, and I suppose the reward was the occasional metallic clang. He also loved to drop stones into the lake at my parents' house. He had a little metal bucket that he'd fill with stones. Then he would tromp up the ramp to the pier where he'd lean over and drop them one by one into the water. They'd make a wonderful "plump, plump, plump" sound. He'd do these things for hours; he was so centered and calm.

There are moments in my life where nothing intrudes, and I feel completely at ease. No fears. No worries. No cares. Those moments "live" in my mind. Years later I can still see them, hear them, smell them. I wonder if it's like that for Ian sometimes—sort of like wine and avocados.

{ 80 }

Corners

I steel myself for the rage like a soldier going into battle. Ian is upset about something in his video game, and I have let it go too long.

Sometimes there is a part of me that is afraid, and as I rise from my chair, moving towards his room, I pass the front door with its promise of escape. I play with the image for a bit, a child eyeing a forbidden sweet.

No more rages, no more days spent walking on eggshells. No more worries about the future, no more autism . . . no more Ian.

No more Ian! The thought leaves me cold and ashamed.

I head down the hallway to his room.

"Ian, you need to come off the game now. You're letting it take control."

"Stupid words, they never work." I mumble to myself.

But this time is different. Ian takes a breath, and as he teeters there on the brink, I see him weigh the choices for the first time.

"Okay," he says with a sigh.

I stand there in the doorway, stunned. He turns off the game, stands up, and wanders from his room to watch a movie.

I return to my chair, pick up the book I'd dropped, and try to find the thread of the story once more, but the words have no hold on me now. The peace I had felt a few moments ago is gone. It has been replaced with a thought that I dare not entertain, for if it isn't true, I doubt I can stand the disappointment. But it dances there in my mind, taunting me with its promise.

Are we turning a corner?

81

Rain and Candlelight

"**W**hy don't you come for the Friday Seminar anymore?" a fellow teacher asked.

We were standing in the teachers' room, it was Friday afternoon, and the regular group was heading out for our occasional "Friday Seminar." Translation: drinks at a local bar.

"I've got to get home to the kids," I said.

"Why don't you get a sitter at least once in a while. We miss you. You're taking this father stuff way too seriously," she added, laughing.

I laughed too, grateful for the chance to make a joke of it, but angry at the same time. She made it sound so easy to just pick up the phone and hire a sitter.

But it's not easy, I thought, feeling my resentment building. *Maybe if we had a normal kid like you. But we don't . . . we've got Ian.*

I got into my car and headed for home. On an impulse, I turned off the highway and drove past the bar. Already, there were a few familiar cars out front. I pictured my friends, drinks in hand, heading towards a table laughing, relaxed, and ready for the weekend to come.

It was starting to rain as I turned back towards the highway. I rolled my window down, my car filled with the cold, wet scent. I love the rain; usually it cheers me, but not that day.

If I lived on the coast, I'd be in the rain and fog all the time, I thought bitterly. But I'm stuck here.

When I arrived home, Michelle and the kids were already there. I opened the door and was immediately hit with the sound of Ian and Kaylee screaming at each other.

Michelle greeted me with a wry smile.

"At least you didn't have to listen to this all the way home," she said.

I mumbled something in response as I pulled off my shoes.

"Steve and Anna are going on a cruise for their tenth wedding anniversary."

"God, that's just great and we're lucky to get a night," I muttered bitterly. "Oh, I know, they don't have to deal with finding a sitter for Ian." I added in response to her look.

"Who would we get to watch him for that long?" Michelle asked, "He wears our parents out."

"Yeah, I know. I'm taking my shower," I said.

As the warm water poured over me, I thought of my friends having drinks at the bar and of Steve and Anna excitedly planning their cruise. I felt alone and overwhelmed.

I dressed slowly, grabbed my book, and headed for the living room. Kaylee puttered by, humming to herself. Ian followed her into our bedroom.

"Where are you guys going?" I asked.

"To watch a movie," Ian said.

Michelle had candles lit and was sitting on the couch reading. I put on some music, poured two glasses of wine, handed one to Michelle, and sank into my chair. It was pouring now, the rain a droning counterpoint to the music. Michelle looked beautiful in the glow of the candles.

I read for a bit and let our companionable silence wash over me in soothing waves. The rain poured on.

The CD ended and I got up to put on another, stopping on the way to check on the kids. They lay there under the covers engrossed in their movie, beautiful faces alight in the glow. The rain hissed against the window in wind-driven gusts.

I returned to my chair, images of cruises and loud bars dissolving into the peace of the rain and the candlelight.

82

Time

"Where's Special Baby?" Ian asked as I was kissing him good night.

"I don't know, Bug. What did you do with her last night?"

It was then that I realized . . . I couldn't remember the last time I'd seen Ian with his doll.

"You haven't been holding her in a while, have you? I haven't even seen you with your Jean either."

Ian looked worried. "You won't throw them away, will you?"

"Don't be silly, Bug."

"Are you going to give them to someone else?" he really sounded upset.

"Oh, Ian . . . of course not. Jean and Baby are too special. We'd never get rid of them."

"What if I don't hold them?"

"Even if you don't hold them anymore. We'll always have them somewhere safe in your room where you can see them."

I found Special Baby and Jean up on his top bunk.

"Do you want them tonight?"

"Yeah," he said snuggling down.

The next morning they were both on the floor beside his bed. I picked them up and carefully set them on his top bunk again.

Next year Ian will turn thirteen. He will be a teenager. My son is growing up, and in a very real way, it makes me sad.

"What does 'E' stand for?" Ian asks.

"Ian, you know the answer. What does 'E' stand for?" We've had this conversation many times before.

He is looking at the advertisement for a video game in his magazine.

" 'E' means everyone can play it."

"Yep, that's right," I say, knowing what will come next.

"What does 'T' mean?"

"What *does* 'T' mean, Ian?"

"'T' means it's for teenagers. What does 'M' stand for?"

"You know the answer."

"'M' is for mature; that's not appropriate for kids."

He rolls the word "appropriate" around on his tongue for a while.

"Next year I'll be a teenager, and I can play teenage games."

"Next year we will *talk* about teenage games. Some will still not be appropriate."

He wanders off then, whispering "appropriate" to himself.

Ian . . . a teenager, I think to myself, shaking my head. *Those years are so hard. How much harder will they be for an autistic?*

Ian's school day begins in the staff parking lot, as it has every day for the past seven years. This is one part of his life that I've missed out on, but I see the images in my mind as though I were there.

"Grab your backpack," Michelle will say.

"Bye Mom!" and Ian is off to the crosswalk.

"I love you!" she says.

"Love you too!" he calls over his shoulder.

"Hi, Ian," says the crossing guard as Ian trudges past, backpack rolling along behind. "Have a good day!"

Then it's off to morning recess for a game of chase, or perhaps wall ball, until the bell rings. Then he heads to class. He has been working with Mrs. Chase for two years now, and he is thriving on the continuity.

At lunch, perhaps I have mixed up his sandwich with Kaylee's yet again, no problem . . . Kaylee will be coming in soon. The switch is made with a hug, and he's off again.

"Hi, Mom!" he'll call on his way out to lunch recess.

And so Ian's days go and he is secure in the simple routine of them. Soon it will all be left behind. He will, for the first time in his life, be alone.

Time marches inexorably forward; change is a necessity of life.

Sometimes I want to scream . . . to scream until my voice is gone, and make it stop.

***

Ian and I stand together at the seaside watching the waves. The air is crisp, cold, and sharp, as only sea air can be. One by one the waves rush up the sand, hissing about our feet before they return to the sea. We throw pieces of driftwood into the water.

I know it will be time for us to go soon, but not yet. A retreating wave reveals a perfectly round stone; Ian picks it up and hands it to me. I put it in my pocket. Another wave rushes in, and as it flows back out again, our feet sink deep into the sand . . . solid and immobile. I take Ian's hand in my own, and I am content.

{ 83 }

Autistic

Yesterday I told you that you are autistic. I watched your face carefully as you slowly rolled that weighted word around your tongue. How strange it was to hear it pass your lips for the first time.

It's just a word, I thought to myself. *Nothing has changed.*

Oh, but it has. The secret, kept from you these twelve long years, is finally out. The label has been given. The word has been placed in your head. Now you must go forth and make it your own.

{ 84 }

The Cereal Aisle

I walked into the Buy and Save market and was instantly transported back nearly 40 years. The place was almost exactly as I remembered it. I was surprised, since the town I grew up in has since become very upscale. I expected fancy cheeses and fine wines. What I found was my childhood.

Mom and I spent a lot of time there—even before I was born.

Mom tells the story often. "They used to see me coming and meet me at the door. I was so huge with you that they were afraid I'd give birth right there in the store. They would practically do my shopping for me."

What I remember most is the cereal aisle in all its sugar-coated glory. From the time I was able to stand on my own, Mom would park me there while she did the rest of the shopping.

"Stay right here," she'd say. "Don't go anywhere, and when I come back, be ready with one box . . . remember, just one."

I'd stand there the entire time Mom was shopping, choosing my week's box of cereal solely by the prize it contained.

Things are so different now. Ian and Kaylee are only allowed to choose a box of sugar cereal at the beginning of vacations and on their birthday week. The thought of leaving them alone in the cereal aisle of the store is unheard of. Even the prizes have changed. There are very few cereal boxes that contain a prize. Most of them offer "free" things that you have to send for in the mail with the inevitable "Yours free plus shipping and handling." That instant gratification is gone.

As I stood there in the Buy and Save market, childhood memories came flooding back to me.

My best friend Chris and I are sneaking off on our bikes around the corner, absolutely forbidden territory, to get a look at Devil's Hairpin. No one knew how it got that name, but it was the steepest, scariest hill in the entire town. It took us months to get up the courage to ride down it: a quarter of the way up at first, then halfway, and finally the whole terrifying hill. I think Chris was the first. We were five-year-old boys screaming in delighted terror as we flew through the heavy summer air; the wind roaring in our ears and our sun-bleached hair ablaze.

The memories flowed through me as I stood in that old familiar place. I smiled to myself, remembering the child I once was. I could almost hear the laughter of summer days, now almost forty years gone.

But as so often happens, my thoughts soon turned to Ian.

Will Ian have memories like this? I thought.

I took a last look at the cereal aisle and its ghosts from my past; then I turned and left.

Since that day I have often wondered if Ian will look back on a childhood full of memories that are rich and vivid? Or will he look back at a colorless, narrow life, which was always constricted by the limits of his autism? As the sadness of that thought fills me, I think of a photograph that sits on my father's desk.

Ian is leaping from the dock into my outstretched arms. We are mainly silhouettes, but the droplets of water flying from his sun-bronzed skin sparkle like jewels. The lake is blue, and life is good. I hear again the laughter of that day, see the wild and wonderful abandon on his face. For Ian, in that moment, there is only me, the lake, and the jewel-filled rush of air . . . nothing else intrudes.

That day will end with the sun. Ian, again a silhouette, pulls a stone from his bucket and drops it into the lake . . . plunk. The ripples spread in perfect circles. He watches them and is glad. The waves lap gently against the shore, a heron calls, and the sun is gone. Ian stands there in the gloaming, so centered and calm.

To live in the moment, with no thoughts of tomorrow and no fear of the future, I think that is the key to a happy life. I believe Ian has found it.

On my dark days, I sometimes think I might trade all of my memories for that kind of peace.

New Air

A gentle breeze stirred the air in the classroom. It was old air, air full of September and the first weeks of school; full of Halloween and Pilgrims; of Christmas with its magic and the excitement of two weeks' vacation. Air full of rainy day recesses and the scent of pencil shavings. Air full of math and reading and spelling, the words hovering there like ghosts; another year was coming to its end.

"He's doing great in math," Mrs. Chase went on, but I wasn't paying attention.

My mind was still back on what she'd said a moment before, words said casually, almost as an afterthought, but words that hung in that weighted, year-old air, spinning there with the math facts and the old spelling words.

"Ian's handling his behavior better. He's learned to take a break outside on his own."

"What does he do out there?" I'd asked.

"Oh, he paces back and forth, counts to ten, stuff like that," Laurie had said.

She continued down his report card, talking about spelling, math, P.E. None of it mattered to me.

He's handling his behavior, I thought.

I feel the breeze again; it tastes of summer, and of the future.

{ 86 }

Summertime

Teaching is a strange profession, especially at the end of the school year. The last few weeks are incredibly busy, emotional, and stressful. Then, suddenly, it's over. It's kind of like climbing a huge mountain, then jumping off the cliff at the top and floating.

I think in many ways it is the same for Ian. In years past, summertime was quite difficult for him. We quickly learned that he is a creature of routine and that he is lost without it. Long before the last day of school arrived, Michelle and I would have Ian's summer schedule worked out in fine detail. But as the years have gone by, Ian has begun to fill up his days on his own. Now I feel he handles the transition better than I do.

"How many more days till summer, Dad?"

Ian asks that question daily from spring break on. As summer vacation approaches, his anticipation grows. The last week of school for Ian is intense. All schedules are out the window as Rocket Day, Field Day, and the end-of-the-year Awards Ceremony follow one another in rapid succession. Finally the last day arrives, and Ian joins me floating in space. We drift there for a while together, feathers on the breeze, lost without the structure of school.

After a few lost days, Ian falls into a pattern. The novelty of sleeping late lasts for a day or two, and then Ian is back to waking up early in the morning. Soon we find that he has pulled out leftover workbooks from school. He works diligently in them for a week or so, and then they are set aside.

His bridge to summer now complete, he settles into a new schedule. Awake by 7:30, he climbs into bed with Michelle and I. The bigger he gets, the more a king-size bed looms in our future. Soon he's off to play his video game for an hour or so, and the morning dwindles away. Then into the pool after lunch, cartoons at 4:30, shower at 6:00. He has learned to quickly find new routines for himself.

I have a harder time of it. My guitar and I become strangers. I don't write, and soon I begin to fear that I never will again. The house projects I had excitedly lined up during the spring seem overwhelming. I watch Michelle and Kaylee. They appear so easy-going and relaxed as they slip easily into what feels to me like a huge void.

And then I see Ian, so like me in many ways, as he happily settles into the new schedule he has made for himself. I follow him, and soon my days are full again.

Nail by nail, our dark kitchen is transformed into a new, bright space, and the living room floor awaits. Pounding nails is a perfect break from teaching.

Soon, evenings are spent with my guitar again, although unlike during the school year, not every evening. I spend just enough time to keep things limber. Just as often, Michelle and I can be found out beneath the stars, reading in the porch light.

And to my great relief, as I settle into my new routine, the words return.

***

I sit in the warm summer night, bathed in the blue glow of my laptop, the clicking of the keys a rhythmic counterpoint to the throbbing drone of the crickets. A soft breeze stirs the leaves of the oaks, bays, and poplars that surround me… a gentle hiss.

I sit here in this beautiful darkness, and I write about my son. My autistic son who led me out into the summer stars.

{ 87 }

Sons

Dinner was over. Mom and I were sitting outside with our coffee.

"Your father's aneurism has grown," she said quietly.

Dad's doctor had discovered an aneurism on his aorta during surgery for a collapsed lung. It was small, so rather than operating, they'd checked it once a year to make sure it wasn't growing. There had been no change for so long that I'd almost forgotten about it.

"What now?" I asked, my mind numb.

"Well, we're not sure. They need to do some more tests, but they might need to operate."

"I thought the doctor said he wouldn't be able to handle anymore surgeries."

"Well, we need to wait and see."

I sat there in the darkness and felt cold despite the August heat. Suddenly I was a child again. I wished that Mom hadn't told me, that she'd chosen to protect her son from the awful realities of life and of my father's advanced age. I heard the screen door close and Michelle's and Dad's voices as they came to join us.

"If anyone can survive a surgery like that, it'd be Dad," I said, trying to sound brave, trying to be a man.

Mom didn't answer.

Later that night, alone in bed with Michelle, the child came back.

Michelle held me tightly as the tears came.

***

"Guys, I need to tell you something," I said at dinner. "Grandpa is having an operation tomorrow."

"In a hospital?" asked Ian.

"Yeah, Bug, that's where they do operations."

"Will he be asleep like when they did my tubes?"

"Yeah."

"Is it a big operation?" Kaylee asked.

"Well, yes it is," I answered.

"Is he scared?" she asked.

"I'm sure he's nervous . . . we all are. But Grandpa is strong."

The questions ended there, but I'm sure the thoughts didn't. The rest of the meal was eaten in silence.

That night I watched Ian for a long time as he slept, wondering if Dad had ever stood like that watching me. Then I went to bed, scared for tomorrow.

On my nightstand is an old silver napkin ring engraved with my father's name. It is a memento from his childhood. I pick it up, stroke it with my thumb, and think of those family dinners all those years ago. Dad was just a boy then . . . still a son.

Sons, and sons, and sons... they drift down to me through the years, parading through my mind that long night as I drift towards sleep.

{ 88 }

Poots

Ian has decided that he is one of the strongest people on earth. To prove this to himself, and to anyone else who may doubt this fact, he has started trying to pick people up. Young or old, big or little, he eyes everyone he meets like an Olympian weightlifter. To him, they are living, breathing dumbbells lined up before him in his quest for a medal.

It is rather startling for the unfortunate victim to be lifted two feet into the air in lieu of a hello. Michelle and I have been diligent in thwarting Ian's attempts, but sometimes he slips through our guard.

***

We were heading out to the car after a visit to Mom and Dad. I was helping Kaylee in her attempts to carry the four hundred or so stuffed animals she always brings along when my suddenly my mother levitated before my eyes.

"Ian, put Grandma down!" I said sternly.

Ian didn't hear. His eyes were bulging—he was going for the gold. Fortunately, Mom was laughing. In fact, she laughed so hard that she passed gas. I was stunned. In forty-two years, I'd never heard nor imagined that my dear mother was capable of such a thing.

Ian was shocked too. He instantly put her back on the ground, a horrified expression on his face.

"Oh, Grandma!" he moaned.

"Grandma pooted, huh?" Ian asked.

We were in the car on our way home.

"Yes, Ian. You can't go around picking people up like that," I said.

"I know. I'll stop."

Silence, and then Ian's voice drifted sotto voce' from the back seat.

"Pooted. Grandma pooted. Poooooted."

Ian's Grandma-lifting days had come to an abrupt end.

***

We sat in the hospital room with my Dad. The surgery was over, and I sat there with Michelle and the kids, basking in the sight of my father. He was alert and joking, healthy and whole. I leaned back in my chair and listened to the sound of my children's voices filling that antiseptic room with life. I watched my beautiful wife leaning against the window, her body framed in the warm September sunlight. And I looked at my father, still with us, and thought about how much I still needed him. I almost felt as though I were five years old again, young and vulnerable, but safe because my Dad was at my side.

Suddenly an unmistakable sound came from the bed. Ian's ears perked up immediately.

"That'll be my ticket out of here," Dad said unabashed. "They won't let me leave until I've gone big poops."

"Grandpa!" Ian cried.

We all laughed, and my mind swept back to Ian and Grandma.

Another sound came from the bed, louder this time.

What a wonderful sound, I thought to myself.

"Pooted. Poooooted. Grandpa pooted," Ian whispered to himself.

89

Video Games

"And what does your son like to do?"

We've been asked this question a million times by many people: doctors, psychiatrists, case workers, friends. I always hesitate before I answer.

"Video games," I say sheepishly.

I hesitate because I am ashamed. Michelle and I hate video games, and we swore that we'd never have one in the house. But that was long ago in the days when our road stretched out before us, smooth and straight as far as the eye could see. That was before we had an autistic son.

Birthdays and Christmases have always been a challenge. A pile of gifts, carefully chosen and brightly wrapped get torn open in excited lightning bursts, their contents spill to the floor where they are soon forgotten.

I can think of few toys that sparked any interest in Ian: Special Baby, a basketball hoop, and the green plastic truck. He was just as interested in odd objects like the washing machine, our vacuum cleaner, or an old rain gutter.

"So, what does Ian want for his birthday this year?"

"He's been asking for a scrap of rain gutter."

Then one day Ian came home with an old Nintendo game system

given to him by his daycare provider. As his obsession grew, more systems inevitably followed until now, to my private shame, he has what he calls his "game office" looming in his bedroom. He would probably sit in there all day hunched in the glow of the screen if we let him, but we quickly set up time restrictions: an hour before dinner on school days, with an hour or so added on weekends.

Ian loves games in which he has to break codes or solve puzzles to reach the next level, and he is quite good at them. He frequently beats a new game within a couple of days. These games are very complex, at least they seem so to someone like me, who thought the game Pong was the height of technological magic. I tell myself that at least his brain is being challenged. And there is another unexpected bonus—

"Where'd you get that guy?"

"You get him in level three if you go to the . . . " Ian launched into an involved description of God knows what.

I turned from watching Kaylee's dance class to find Ian talking with a slightly younger boy whom I'd never seen before. They were talking about a game Ian was playing on his Game Boy.

"I haven't made it to that level yet," the boy said.

"It's easy. I'll show you," Ian replied.

I smiled as I watched the two of them huddled over the small screen. Just two boys lost in a common interest.

I sat back in my chair and watched my son. Ian on equal ground with a "normal" kid, his autism, for the moment, forgotten.

90

The Toss of a Coin

Rage and innocence . . .
light and dark.
I see the four of us carefully walking that narrow,
twisting line between the Yin and the Yang.
Two faces of the same coin . . . two sides of my son.
Over the years that coin has been tossed a million times.
We have watched as it flies into the air,
a spinning silver blur until it falls to the ground
and spins to a stop.
The years pass us by, and more and more...
it comes up heads.

91

The Spelling Bee

Unlike many kids his age, Ian never swears. I'm not saying he's naïve; he knows all the words— all of the biggies, plus a few more. He just never says them. Instead he spells them.

"Dad, today at school David said the 'H' word. Why do kids like to say those words?"

"Because they think it makes them sound cool. I'm glad you don't say them."

"They think they sound like high-schoolers, huh? David said the 'S' word too. You know, s-@-#-*.' "

"Ian, you don't have to spell it. I know which word you're talking about."

"The 'H' word is h-@-&-*.' "

"I know, Bug. Please don't spell them; it's almost like saying them."

"He said the 'D' word too. That's spelled . . . "

It's a lost cause. I suppose I could give him consequences for spelling them. I would if he ever came up to me screaming, "Dad, you are a big, ugly S#$%!" But as things stand now, I don't have the heart, especially after last week.

The phone rang in my classroom during my fifth-grade band class.

"I know you're in the middle of class, but I had to tell you . . . he won!" Michelle was practically yelling into the phone.

It took me a bit to realize she was talking about Ian. Ian was his class's representative in the school spelling bee. We'd had three days to help him study during a three-day weekend trip to Lake Tahoe. He had barely looked at the list.

"You're kidding!"

"He's going on to the county spelling bee in two weeks! He's representing the whole school!"

I hung up the phone in a proud daze.

"If they give him swear words, he'll have it nailed," I mumbled to myself as I went back to my band.

Later that day, I sat at my desk looking at his picture. He stared back at me with his toothy grin, his blonde hair, and his soulful eyes. To look at him, you'd never know he was autistic—how far he has come against such great odds. You'd never know that it took six years of intense work before he was able to carry on a conversation. You would never imagine the horribly violent rages he used to throw, or the fearful sorrow that followed. You'd never know how hard he works to have the few friends he does and the disappointments he endures watching his sister blossom into such a popular girl. You'd never know how many people give him strange looks or how often he is the butt of a cruel joke.

I don't know how he'll do in the county spelling bee, and I don't really care. It will be enough just to watch as he walks out onto that stage and to think about all he has had to overcome to be able to take those steps.

92

A Fish Story

"Dad, something's wrong with Osa," Ian said.

Something's going to be wrong with you if you don't get into bed was what I wanted to say. Instead, "I'll come look."

Getting Ian into bed that night had been like pulling teeth. He'd managed to find every conceivable excuse to delay the inevitable, and as I followed him into his room, all I wanted to do was check the damn fish as quickly as possible so he'd go to sleep.

Osa was belly up in the tank; his glassy eyes stared at me accusingly.

"You're right, Ian," I said, feeling a bit guilty. "Osa is dead."

Goldfish are the ultimate in disposable pets, and I thought nothing of it as I scooped him from the tank.

"Yuck, I don't want to see him." Ian moaned as I walked past.

I headed into the bathroom, dropped Osa in the toilet, and flushed. Ian was quiet as he watched Osa spin out of sight.

I was checking our email when Ian walked in. I looked up, angry that he was out of bed yet again.

"IAN . . . " I started to say, but the words died in my throat when I saw the look on his face.

"I'm sad about Osa, but I'm not going to cry," Ian said, swallowing hard.

"Come here, let's sit on the couch and talk," I said.

We walked into the living room. I moved some papers out of the way and sat down. Ian sat down beside me.

"Why did he die, Dad?"

"I guess it was just his time, Bug," I said.

"Where is he now?" Ian asked, with a glance towards the bathroom.

"Are you worried about me flushing him?" I asked. *STUPID!* I thought, *What were you thinking, flushing his fish?*

He just looked at me with his deep brown eyes. They were filling up now, salty oceans of tears.

"You know that movie, *Finding Nemo*?" I asked.

He was a step ahead of me.

"You mean all drains lead to the sea?" he asked, quoting the film.

"Yeah. Fish don't like to be buried in the ground like hamsters. They want to go to the sea."

"Will a shark eat him?"

"Sharks don't like to eat dead fish," I said.

"Will he just sink and get buried in the sand?"

"Yeah, Bug, just like that."

"Maybe he'll turn into a new fish," he said hopefully.

"Well, I don't know about that, but if he does, he'll probably be any kind of fish he wants."

"I think he'll turn into a dolphin, 'cause dolphins always beat sharks," Ian said.

I had a momentary vision of a group of dolphins, Osa in the lead, leaping into the air from deep blue waters, droplets scattering amidst flashes of sunlight. They leaped again and again, wild and free.

I said, "You know it's okay to cry. I cry . . . all the time."

He took a shuddering breath. "Like when I won that award in second grade. You cried then, huh?"

"Yeah, Bug, those were happy tears. I also cry when I'm sad. That doesn't make me weak . . . it makes me strong."

"I don't want to cry."

"Well, if you decide to, it's okay. It's a good thing to cry sometimes. You want me to come snuggle with you for a while?"

"Okay."

I lie there in the soft darkness with Ian by my side. . . my twelve-year-old son whose wondrously deep soul is able to care so much for something as simple as a goldfish. Soft, beautiful, and full of sleep, his lullaby tape plays quietly in the background, as it has almost every night of his life.

"Do you want Jean and Baby?" I ask.

"Okay."

"You know they're on your top bunk whenever you need them."

"I know," he says, his body softening a bit as he pulls them close.

We lie in silence for a while, and I stroke his hair, strands of gold fall through my fingers—his breathing slows.

"I love you, Bug," I whisper into the scent of him, pulling him close.

"I love you too, Dad."

***

My family has come a long way together, but we still have far to go. The path stretches away as far as I can see. It will be full of hidden beauty and bitter tears, wondrous joy and painful truths, and we will walk it together, the four of us, lending each other strength along the way.

At the bottom of all the questions and all the doubts and the fears, I know one thing, and it is a thing of great worth. A wonderful gift has come into my family.

It is a gift full of sweet innocence and magical childlike wonder. It is a gift of laughter and wondrous rivers of cleansing tears. It is the magic of sharing sadness at the death of a fish . . . it is Ian.

I love my son with my entire heart and soul, with every ounce of strength and will that I possess . . .

I am a better man for having Ian in my life.

***

ABOUT THE AUTHOR

Hank Smith is an elementary school teacher living in Northern California. Living with his son, Ian, has been an amazing learning experience which has not only helped him in working with children with special needs at his school, but also has given him valuable insight to share with parents and educators. Hank and Ian share their story in well-received talks, workshops, and keynote addresses throughout California. **Sticks and Stones** is his first book.

CPSIA information can be obtained at www.ICGtesting.com
Printed in the USA
LVOW07s1552190615

443146LV00002B/270/P